Praise for Jordan Kemper and *Red Key Revolution*

"In *Red Key Revolution*, Jordan will give you the road map for constant learning, improvement, and reinvention of yourself every day to make sure your life is rich with significance."

—Tony Jeary, The RESULTS Guy™,
author, and coach to the world's top CEOs

"Life is so short. Jordan's book will have you on the edge of your seat, motivated to make the most of every moment, starting now."

—Jon Vroman, founder of FrontRowFoundation.org
and author of *The Front Row Factor*

"*Red Key Revolution* will show you how to take those extra steps beyond success. Significance is about the lives we can touch and the legacy we can leave."

—Ted DiBiase Jr., former WWE Wrestler, actor,
and Vice President, One Life America

"Jordan's genuine passion and gift for inspiring people is captured in *Red Key Revolution*. It will help you evaluate your goals, discover what actually matters to you, and ultimately help you live your best life. As an athlete, I am constantly trying to improve my mental game. This book has helped shed light on what success really means and how I can systematically improve my approach to achieving it."

—Meaghan Mikkelson Reid, three-time Olympic Medalist
and World Champion, Women's Hockey

"Jordan brings to light real issues we all face in life's journey. His transparency about his real struggle to live a life of significance will inspire many."

—Craig Altman, Lead Pastor, Grace Family Church

"*Red Key Revolution* is a story of learning how to overcome serving yourself and start dedicating your life to helping others. Jordan's ability to walk-the-walk, and share his experience on how to reach beyond yourself to serve others is explored in his book through his personal journey and life lessons learned. This book's lessons and stories—his and others—create a pathway to a more selfless, compassionate, and noble life."

—Paul Anderson, CEO of Port Tampa Bay,
Presidential appointee to the Federal Maritime Commission

"When it comes to living a life of success, Jordan is someone many people look up to. What sets his message apart is that his key to success is not wrapped up in wealth or power, but in service and significance. It's a much needed reminder that life is not about what we're living for—but *who* we're living for. If you are looking to live a life of significance, this book is for you!"

—Debra Fileta, M.A., LPC, author of *Choosing Marriage*,
and creator of TrueLoveDates.com

"You are designed by God for greatness and a purpose. *Red Key Revolution* reveals how to unlock the greatness within you and to live a life of significance."

—Dr. Dave Braun and Dr. Troy Amdahl, "The OolaGuys,"
best-selling authors, and co-founders of OolaLife.com

"One of the many things serving in Special Operations taught me is when you want to acquire a specific skillset, it's important that you learn from the best teachers in that field. I've known Jordan for five years, and he is one of the best communicators, leaders, friends, and dealmakers that I've encountered. Simply put, he's the best. So for those seeking to learn how to consistently make the best decisions in life, look no further; *Red Key Revolution* is where you'll find your answers—and lessons that will be with you for the rest of your life."

—Remi Adeleke, former Navy SEAL, actor, and author

"*Red Key Revolution:* A movement built on the simple yet revolutionary truth that we are the sum of all our choices. Counter-cultural? Absolutely. Wise? Beyond measure. Instructive? Every step of the way! Dare to read these pages—be part of this powerful movement. Not only will it change your life but the countless lives you have yet to touch!"

—Pam Jordan Wolf, author, speaker, and business success coach

"This amazing little book is a treasure and secret shortcut to personal and professional growth."

—Patricia Rossi, NBC Daytime's
National Etiquette Correspondent

"I love this book. Jordan Kemper is a powerful and imaginative storyteller, and every story has a lesson that will inspire you to become a more confident and powerful person. Jordan's distinction for living a life of love and growth shows in the tens of thousands of lives that he has changed by his words, his heart, and his example. If you ever get a chance to hear him live, make it happen. You will be forever changed."

—Richard Bliss Brooke, author of *Mach 2: The Art of Vision and Self-Motivation* and *The Four Year Career*

"*Red Key Revolution* eloquently lays out what really matters for meaningful significance: a lasting legacy. In the "instant" world we live in, where the focus is on the immediate, Jordan disrupts that paradigm into the long-game perspective and the lasting impact that all of us should pay vastly more attention to. Thanks, Jordan, for your inspiration to me!"

—John J. Koehler, MD, founder, Physicians Immediate Care

"*Red Key Revolution* is a refreshing read in a world obsessed with material success, rather than lasting significance. Jordan Kemper doesn't pull punches, and shoots straight on what it takes to achieve real significance. If you want a life that truly matters, then I challenge you to read this book and apply the principles to your life. It just may be the 'key' you need that unlocks your significance."

—J Leman, NFL veteran, sports broadcaster, and entrepreneur

"In today's immediate gratification culture, it's truly rare to hear of a story like Jordan Kemper's. His book highlights how intentional, others-focused decisions really can be like making cuts to shape your very own key of life; to open or close doors to your future. You won't take lightly the opportunity to make principled decisions again. Read this book for yourself; give this book to your teenagers!"

—Dr. Steve Hryszczuk, anesthesiologist and author

Redefining Success for a Life of Significance

RED KEY
REVOLUTION

JORDAN KEMPER

Foreword by John Bevere

GREENLEAF
BOOK GROUP PRESS

Published by Greenleaf Book Group Press
Austin, Texas
www.gbgpress.com

Distributed by Greenleaf Book Group

For ordering information or special discounts for bulk purchases, please contact Greenleaf Book Group at PO Box 91869, Austin, TX 78709, 512.891.6100.

Design and composition by Greenleaf Book Group
Cover design by Greenleaf Book Group
Cover image copyright bicubic, 2018. Used under license
from Shutterstock.com; Social media icons designed by BiZkettE1/Freepik;
Padlock icon designed by Freepik from Flaticon"

Publisher's Cataloging-in-Publication data is available.

Print ISBN: 978-1-62634-547-8

eBook ISBN: 978-1-62634-548-5

Part of the Tree Neutral® program, which offsets the number of trees consumed in the production and printing of this book by taking proactive steps, such as planting trees in direct proportion to the number of trees used: www.treeneutral.com

Printed in the United States of America on acid-free paper

18 19 20 21 22 23   10 9 8 7 6 5 4 3 2 1

First Edition

To the love of my life, Kristen.
This book is for you.

CONTENTS

FOREWORD

I am honored to call Jordan a friend. He and his wife, Kristen, are both amazing leaders with a passion for helping people. They leave an impact on everyone they meet because they've captured what it means to truly care. He's more concerned with his team's well-being than their business's bottom line. Their driving desire is to see others' lives transformed.

Jordan is a man of great conviction and discipline. When he sets out to make something happen, he has a plan to get there and doesn't waver from it. When he was in middle school, he made a commitment to stay pure until marriage. Despite being mocked and even rejected because of his decision to wait, he stood firm. Jordan married Kristen when he was thirty-one years old, having kept his commitment to God to stay pure. This did not happen by accident—it took years of intentional decision-making.

Too often we focus on what we want now, in the moment, rather than over the long term. We sacrifice greatness for mediocrity, all because it seems easier in the moment. The key of wisdom that unlocks our life's potential is set aside, even tossed away, by our desire for instant gratification. We ultimately create a key that will only open doors that produce long-term disappointments. Bottom line—we decide what door we'll pass through by the way we live.

To make a good cut (decision) in your key, it is so import-ant that we use our head, our heart, and our hands. I've seen Jordan live this out. He makes a sound decision, with the right motives, and works hard to see it through. The insight he pro-vides gives inspiring and practical ways to unlock the kind of life worth living.

I'm so grateful Jordan wrote this book and am confident that these pages will inspire and challenge you to make the right decisions, with the right intentions. As a result, great blessings will follow.

John Bevere
Best-selling Author and Minister
Cofounder of Messenger International

ACKNOWLEDGMENTS

Writing a book is a massive project. Without these people, there would be no words to write and not even a story to tell. It takes many contributors, and I am but one of them.

To my wife, Kristen: You are the inspiration for this book. You were worth the long wait. You were the answer to my prayers, and I know that God will use us together in ways we could never imagine. My red key forever belongs to you.

To my mom and dad: I am who I am today because of you. You taught me to love God and love others by your actions, not just your words. I am proud to be your son. Thank you for a firm foundation and your unconditional love.

To Conn and Christie: I couldn't ask for better siblings. As kids, and now adults, I am so thankful for our unique relationships. You are both so gifted. Thank you for your endless support and encouragement. You have always been my front-row fans.

To Bob and Donna: Thank you for raising Kristen with so much love and intentionality. She is more than I deserve. I promise to love her until my last breath.

To Nate and Jamie: You both pushed me to go beyond what's comfortable. You expected me to see beyond myself. You cast a vision and created a lane for me to run in. You were the catalyst for this movement. I am forever grateful.

To my youth pastor, Brian: Thank you for speaking life into me as a thirteen-year-old boy. You changed my life with one red key, and I promise to multiply your impact.

To my friends: Thank you for standing with Kristen and me. We couldn't have asked God for more loyal and true friends. You have each played a big role in our lives and we love you.

To our Lord Jesus Christ: All glory belongs to You. Every thought, every word, and every story is only possible because of You. You love us all and know us better than we know ourselves. You know who needs this message, and I trust You to deliver it.

START HERE . . .

All keys unlock something. Tangible things, like cars and houses. And intangible things, like solutions and hearts. Sometimes keys unlock life itself.

In varying degrees, a key is a symbol of all forces that open and close, bind and release. It stands for liberation and incarceration. It gives us a sense of security and control. It provides us with access and protection. Keys are one of the most commonly manufactured metal objects in the entire world, and to doubt their importance means you've forgotten about the minor panic attacks that ensue when you realize you forgot them.

Keys can be traced back some six thousand years to ancient Babylon and Egypt. Bulky, heavy, toothbrush-shaped wooden keys went through a hole in the door to move aside a wooden bolt but ultimately proved susceptible to external brute-force attacks. Ancient Greeks were the first to create keys out of metal—giant items that were worn on the shoulder—followed by engineers in ancient Rome who simplified the concept by decreasing the size and reconfiguring the iron and bronze into a cylindrical shaft with one single, thin, and rectangular tooth, known today as a "skeleton key." That design continued for seventeen centuries after the fall of the Roman Empire.

The Industrial Revolution furthered the complexity and sophistication of keys and locks until an American father and son perfected them in the mid-1800s. Linus Yale, Sr. created a lock design that used pins of varying lengths to prevent the lock from opening without the correct key. Twenty years later Linus Yale, Jr., who was inspired by the original pin-tumbler lock designed by his father, patented a small flat key with serrated edges that worked with pins of varying lengths within the lock itself. It's the same design of the pin-tumbler locks, or Yale locks, that remain in use today, and it's what brings me to my next point.

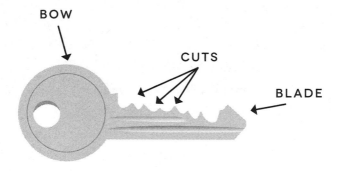

The anatomy of a key is systematic and crucial to its effectiveness. It has two major parts: the blade and the bow. The blade is what slides into the keyway of the lock and distinguishes it from different keys. The bow is left protruding so that torque can be applied by the user. When the correct key is in place, you can turn the cylinder freely and open the lock;

with the wrong key inserted, the cylinder refuses to turn and the lock stays shut. What constitutes the wrong key? The most important parts of all.

The cuts.

Cuts are the grooves on the key blade that align with the internal components of the lock. The series of cuts, produced with the utmost precision by a locksmith, strategically syncs with both the key pins and the spring-loaded pins within the lock to allow you to rotate the key. Like I said, systematic. If one cut is off, it impacts the effectiveness of the key. Sometimes you can jimmy the lock if you're lucky. Or, if you're trying to open a door, you might be able to break it down, which, suffice to say, tends to leave some damage. But if multiple cuts are off, your key won't work. Not a chance. If there's a problem with the cuts, the key's value diminishes.

How do locksmiths know what cuts to make? There's a licensed key code with thousands of alphanumeric character combinations that guide the correct cut. Thousands of tiny incisions that, when made correctly, produce a key that successfully unlocks what's meant to be unlocked.

Now consider this: the Latin root of the word *incision*—meaning "to cut"—is the same root for the word *decision*. Incision means "to cut into" and decision means "to cut off." When you make a decision, you literally cut off the alternative choices in the same way the locksmith removes alternative uses of the key with each additional cut. By making a decision—really making it—you cut off the possibility of anything other than what you've committed to. You remove what is not significant to you in order to make room for what is. If your life has a master key, all you need are the right cuts to unlock greater significance. This book will help you determine what those cuts are.

Why am I calling it a revolution? Because what I say in here is going to challenge some fundamental beliefs you have about your decisions. It's intended to spark a critical conversation that compels you to reexamine your thoughts, actions, and pursuits in order to figure out what you really want from life, why you want it, and how you're going to grab hold of it. I want you to unlock a more significant life; to get there, however, you're going to need to make the cuts that form the key, not me.

When it comes to decision-making, there are two primary parts: your head and your heart. Your head is what transforms what you see, experience, and learn into logic that you can apply to your daily life. The heart goes deeper. It takes what you see, experience, and learn and translates it into meaning; it makes you *feel*. Together, your head and heart compose an eighteen-inch continuum that guides your reasoning, your beliefs, and the subsequent paths you commit to. But decision-making is useless without action.

Therein lies the third part of decision-making: your hands.

Hands are where the action lives. They grab hold or let go and produce tangible follow-through. When all three—head, heart, and hands—come together, you create a cut in your key of life. Enough of the right cuts and you can unlock the life you really want.

At the end of each chapter, I present insights, pose questions, and suggest actions that align your head, heart, and hands to make the right cuts. By the end of the book, you will have the opportunity to make seven cuts that fully form your life key.

At some point, you might find yourself arguing that a certain cut is fine and your key is working perfectly. Maybe it's true. But I'd still ask you to consider that after years and years of use, your cuts can become dull and in need of sharpening in order to continue working effectively. Maybe this book is your opportunity to figure out where life has worn down certain decisions you've made. If so, use this book to sharpen those decisions and affirm the shape of your key.

At this point, you might ask what makes me an expert in keys. I'm really only an expert in red keys—one red key in particular. Now I see all keys that matter as red.

One Wednesday evening at church when I was thirteen years old, the youth pastor gave a talk on what he called "sexual purity." From the stage, he explained abstinence and accountability and why remaining celibate until marriage was the wisest path. Then he held up a red key. It looked like a house key. He said he was giving one to each of us in the audience.

"I challenge you to keep this red key," he explained, "and let it be a symbol of your commitment to wait until marriage." The idea was that we'd give the key to our spouse on our wedding day as a symbol that we saved ourselves for them.

A red key. If only all the important decisions we made came with an aptly colored, tangible reminder of the sacrifices that lie ahead. As a newly minted teen, with all the raging hormones and tenacious curiosities that come with the territory, I can say with certainty that I had little idea what I was doing when I accepted that key. I understood the concept—don't have sex until I'm married—but I didn't have a clue what that would entail or what it would come to mean if

I succeeded. I don't even know that I liked girls all that much at that point.

After my pastor passed out the keys, the other middle schoolers and I all left, and I guarantee most of the kids lost their key within twenty-four hours. Not me. I was all about goals, and this was a new goal to hit, a box to check, a prize to win. I had a safe with a combination lock in a secret drawer in my bedroom and that's where the key would live, evidence of a future victory. While I might not have comprehended the deeper meaning, I knew that someone I respected said I should accept a particular challenge. And I didn't back down from challenges. I also hadn't had a girlfriend yet, so the prospect of meeting the challenge seemed easy enough.

The main thing I knew back then was that the red key meant sacrifice. Giving up one thing for something else. I understood that concept, generally speaking, because I understood the concept of giving up my time or money or fun to become a better athlete. What I didn't yet comprehend was that this sacrifice I was being asked to make *involved* me but was ultimately not *about* me. It also wasn't about things; it was about people. I've since learned—through a lot of trial and error—that this is the best sort of sacrifice to make. It is also the most challenging. Most people shy away like I did for the better part of my life.

We all inevitably sacrifice something to get where we want to go. In other words, we all make cuts to our life key. The question is, are we making the right cuts? We find the answer by looking at what they currently unlock. A thriving business and a failing marriage? A lot of big ideas but little to show for them? A successful career and a life of significance?

Unfortunately, the last combination isn't very common. It wasn't present in my life for a long time, and even today I'm striving to do better. If you're reading this book, I'm guessing you're after something similar.

As I grew up, the symbolism of that original red key started to morph into other areas of my life until it became something of a north star. So, while my first introduction to a red key revolved around the uncomfortable topic of sexuality, I now know that red keys are bigger than one decision in one aspect of our lives. They are the sums of our decisions throughout our lives. This is a book about (1) the challenges we face in keeping the most important decisions we make, (2) the most important sacrifices you can commit to making today, and (3) how it all comes down to following through with the right cuts. In the end, this is also a book about the rewards that accompany the right cuts. They are more desirable, more beautiful, and more meaningful because they unlock a more fulfilling and impactful life.

Let's start discussing what I mean.

REDIRECT YOUR GRATIFICATION

Cut #1: Cut the Selfie

I was born in Rockford, Illinois, just outside of Chicago during Michael Jordan's rookie year with the Bulls, which meant I was one of many local kids who hoped to achieve professional basketball success through osmosis. At ten years old, I was playing 180 games a year on a travel team with players who were mostly older and bigger than me. An average-sized kid with an average athletic ability, I felt pretty on par with them, like I was holding my own. Until.

On a seemingly average day playing a game of shirts and skins, my basketball coach took me aside and grabbed some baby fat on my stomach. He just pulled at it in front of my teammates. I was all-at-once shocked, shy, and sad as I stood there with my bare torso. Did he know that he held in his fingers not just my fat but my pride?

To say I was embarrassed is an understatement; in that moment, I wasn't good enough, wasn't worthy, wasn't as talented or successful as the other athletes. With the type of feigned confidence that only comes with mortification, I held my head up high enough to finish practice and then went home feeling broken. Ashamed. I woke up early the next morning and went to the local track and ran two miles before school. And that was my routine from that day forward. Two miles. Every single day. Before school. Ten years old. It was the end of average.

Along with my evolved exercise habits came a shift in my mindset, in which I became hyperaware of my personal responsibility to the outcome. Input/output, cause/effect, action/reaction, me/me.

Are you surprised that a kid in mid-'90s suburbia—before exposure to the Internet, social media, or *The Biggest Loser*—would have such insight or take such drastic measures for self-improvement? Don't be.

Our nation's interest in personal health and well-being surged in the 1960s and 1970s. Social movements like vegetarianism, natural health, and aerobic exercise went from being on the fringe of pop culture to suddenly defining it, from casual public conversation to deliberate public consumption. The decades rolled on, and with them an evolving mania, until the private practices we used to better ourselves in our day-to-day lives were as mainstream as they were prioritized. Soon, we became a nation obsessed with "self-care."

Self-care can be defined as the responsibility we have for our own well-being and the action we take to ensure it. It's being aware of our choices and selective about which ones we make in order to keep ourselves healthy in body, mind, and spirit. These choices span the spectrum from treadmills to meditation to facials to medicine, and can be personalized to cater to our specific needs. We have so much at our disposal these days.

Unprecedented good has come from the self-care epidemic, in both the personal and societal senses. Strides in consistent exercise, combating addiction, and conscientious eating combined with the leaps and bounds of modern medicine have made human longevity one of the greatest achievements of the modern era. In fact, the United Nations goes as far as to say it's one of the most significant social transformations of the twenty-first century.[1]

No doubt we've come a long way. But at what cost? Fifty years after the initial surge and our obsession has turned against us in some respects. It didn't happen overnight. It happened one personal choice at a time, multiplied. As affirmations became popular, like "Do your thing" and "Take your stand" and "Make time for you," self-care slowly became both an acceptable and sound personal growth strategy. I have to believe the original intent was for people to realize they had the power to change their results, which would make empowerment the expected outcome. But what it led to is decidedly more dramatic.

Ever so slowly, self-care was taken out of context until people elevated it to an entitlement, a right. We owe it to ourselves. We deserve it. Right now. We sacrifice vital elements

---

1   United Nations, Department of Economic and Social Affairs, Population Division, World Population Ageing 2015, ST/ESA/SER.A/390 (2015).

of our lives to maintain the regimens we feel we need. We go to extreme—and often expensive—lengths to reward ourselves with what we feel we've earned. We allow it to take precedence over our scheduled responsibilities. We fight for it, expect it, insist on it, at all costs.

Am I saying self-care isn't important? Not a chance. Taking care of ourselves is a necessity, especially for hardworking individuals who want to succeed at the highest level. I'm in the business of self-care and will shout from the rooftops that eating well, staying fit, taking vitamins, and getting enough rest have been and always will be critical to prosperous health. Asking whether or not self-care is important is the wrong question; the right question is *Why is it important?* Why do we want to take care of ourselves? Why do we want to be healthy? Why do we want to improve ourselves? What's the motivation behind it?

If you went one by one around a gym and asked people why they were there, why they prioritized their workout on that particular day, you'd get an array of answers. And they'd probably all be perfectly reasonable.

"My high school reunion is coming up, and I want to stick it to the mean girls."

"I entered the strongman contest, and I don't want to embarrass myself."

"I have a crush on a personal trainer, and I'm trying to get face time."

"It's how I keep my sanity and stay patient with my kids."

"I'm rehabilitating my ankle and want to get back to the team."

"My doctor says thirty minutes of cardio a day will help lower my cholesterol."

Each one is an equation of sorts: Behavior = Intention + Motivation. But the last three examples above? The difference is in the why.

My routine of an early morning alarm clock and subsequent eight laps around the track each day was established so I could run farther and faster than my teammates, jump higher and be more agile, score more points, and get more rebounds. Why? I wanted to prove my coach wrong and be recognized as the best person on my team. I was willing to forgo sleep and energy to attain these feats, to make up for my lack of raw talent by outworking everybody; I equated sacrifice with accomplishment. The day my coach grabbed my belly fat was the last day he would have something to criticize.

"Pinch me, I dare you," is what the chip on my shoulder would have said if it could talk.

If it sounds like I was angry or bitter, I'm missing the mark. The belly-fat incident was pivotal in that it was the fuel that stoked the fire inside me—a fire I was grateful to have. I found purpose in my quest for achievement because at the end was affirmation. Having a reason to work toward a goal meant that I was taking initiative to ensure no one would count me out again.

Have you had a belly-fat moment in your life? Did it propel you forward or pull you back?

That incident is when my cycle of prioritizing self-care for self-gain began. I became fixated on setting goals—a mindset that is apparent in a formal list in my fifth-grade notebook.

What could I accomplish next? What could I check off? What did I need to endure to help myself achieve it?

- ☐ Be middle school valedictorian
- ☐ Be homecoming king
- ☐ Be high school valedictorian
- ☐ Be a top basketball scorer in the state of Illinois
- ☐ Play college basketball
- ☐ Be a medical doctor

Ready, set, reach.

Achievement of these personal goals would require hard work, resilience, and dedication. My all-in mentality thrived on the idea of them, and I didn't flinch at the long, laborious tasks I'd have to endure in order to accomplish them. Challenge accepted.

My alarm clock started going off even earlier. Though I was a good student, it didn't come as naturally to me as it did to others, so I would wake up at 4:30 a.m. to study. Much of the time that meant reading. I wasn't a good reader, and in order to make no room for error, I would read everything twice. And then I would head to the track to run my two miles.

When I look back on it, what's so troubling wasn't the go-getter attitude of my adolescent self (I mean, who would fault a kid for taking an active role in bettering himself?) but the self-serving nature of it. It had nothing to do with bettering the team and everything to do with proving that I was the best athlete. It wasn't about studying science and history so I could tutor other kids; it was so I would get an A on the test and be looked upon as the smartest kid in the class. I was hooked on the glory, which in my mind I had twisted to be a good thing, a noteworthy nod to my hard work, the affirmation that I was maximizing my potential.

Years later when I played high school basketball, I would forgo going out with the team after games on Friday nights so that I could go home and record local postgame newscasts on VHS to track how many times I was talked about. On Saturday mornings I rewatched the broadcasts to hear my name and relive how many points and rebounds and accolades I got. Then I would open the *Rockford Register Star* to see it in print. Print lived forever.

It's safe to say my self-care had morphed into self-gratification. What's the difference? If self-care is taking care of ourselves, then self-gratification is the indulgence of those actions. There's a fine line between the two that many of us cross unknowingly.

Self-gratification, inherently, is selfish. It's gratifying one's own impulses, needs, or desires, often at the expense of others. The polar opposite is sacrifice—true, virtuous sacrifice is at our own expense for the sake of others. The focus on doing it for others' sake is especially imperative because even though I sacrificed things like sleep, time, and energy on the road to accomplishing my list of goals, it was all for my sole benefit. If my actions had a positive effect on others, it was an unplanned and convenient side effect of my mission to be the best.

That's not to say I was completely unable to genuinely sacrifice or care for others.

My younger sister, Christie, used to have trouble sleeping. Rather than sleep in my own room in my own bed, I slept in the twin bed next to hers, because I thought that if she didn't feel alone, if she knew someone was there to support her, she might have an easier time falling asleep and getting a good night's rest. And I felt great when she did. It didn't matter to me that I actually didn't sleep well in there—I preferred it was me and not her who was up during the night. Her win was my win. Still, that version of self-care—the other-centered kind— wasn't the main scene in my life. I didn't get it yet.

Ultimately, gratification is determined by what motivates us: self or others. If we live for ourselves and only care about what we're going through and what we have and how our lives are going, our gratification is based on that. If we live for others and put their needs before our own and desire to see them achieve success, our gratification is based on that.

Puritan philosopher Jonathan Edwards's view of free will is that we are free to choose but are ultimately a slave to our greatest desire. And the apostle Paul said that through our actions each day we are either pleasing the desires of our flesh or the desires of our spirit. We can't please both at the same time. Each one can lead us down a path to success, but the success would be measured differently—by what we got or what we gave.

For much of my adolescent, teen, and young adult life, I was aiming to get. I didn't understand how good—no, how much better—it felt to take actions that pleased my spirit over my surface desires. For most of that time, my greatest desires revolved around the promotion of my own agenda. There was nothing wrong with my goals, but because I was a slave to them, I wasn't yet capable of the higher order of ambitions.

When my parents were first married, my dad decided to start his own business. He didn't want to be accountable to a boss who dictated his hours and priorities, and he reasoned that if he was self-employed, it would allow him the opportunity to be the husband and (eventual) father he wanted to be. Nose to the grindstone, he worked eighteen-hour days and made certain sacrifices with his time and attention in order to build a strong foundation for his business.

When my mom and dad started having kids, he cut back his hours. He turned down jobs instead of continuing to develop the company and said no to bigger and better ventures because the personal cost would have been too great. His motivation for starting the business and putting in the level of effort he did in the beginning was to afford him the freedom of being a present and involved husband and father when the time came.

Did he miss out on more money, more acclaim, or more professional growth? One-hundred-percent yes. But he'd tell you he wasn't surrendering anything important. His joy was found in fulfilling his role as our father—being there when we woke up in the morning and got home from school, helping us with our homework, and getting to be our coach. The choices he made early on were driven by his desire to care for us well; it was for our benefit, and his gratification was a natural by-product. Jonathan Edwards would say my dad was a slave to his desire for us to thrive.

What happens when the highest level of success in our personal endeavor requires regularly putting others' needs before our own? Isn't there a conflict? We don't like to admit that—in fact, many won't—but it's true. To fully commit to meeting others' needs requires thinking and doing for others before we think and do for ourselves. It often requires prioritizing others' needs and delaying the gratification of our own. Daily.

The concept of delayed gratification was put to the test in the 1960s when a professor from Stanford University conducted a series of psychological studies on children that he called the "marshmallow experiment."

A child was brought into a private room, seated in a chair, and had a marshmallow placed on the table in front of him or her. The child was told that if he or she did not eat the marshmallow while the researcher was away, he or she would be rewarded with a second marshmallow. However, if the child decided to eat it before the researcher came back, he or she would not get a second marshmallow.

The choice was simple: one treat now or two treats later. The researcher left the room for fifteen minutes.

Some kids jumped up and ate the first marshmallow as soon as the researcher closed the door. Others wiggled and bounced and scooted in their chairs as they tried to restrain themselves, but eventually gave in to temptation a few minutes later. And a few of the children managed to wait the entire time.

What's perhaps most interesting about the experiment is what the researchers learned when they conducted follow-up studies and tracked each child's progress. The children who delayed their gratification by waiting to receive the second marshmallow ended up having higher SAT scores, lower levels of substance abuse, a lower likelihood of obesity, and better responses to stress, among other positive results.[2]

It's an interesting demonstration of how success can come down to choosing the pain of discipline over the ease of capitulation or practicing self-control instead of succumbing to instant gratification—mastering patience for the hope of a bigger and better prize.

But how about this scenario: What if there had been no prize, no promise of a second marshmallow for the child to eat? Instead, what if the child was told that by not eating the first marshmallow, the reward would be that he or she got to give the second marshmallow to a loved one? Would he or she have resisted the temptation without the incentive of personal gain? Would you?

No one ever said sacrifice was easy.

What would happen if we learned to find gratification in something only others could give us? If our mindfulness for them not only preceded our actions but determined them. If we did things based on what they would get out of it instead of what we would get out of it. That sort of strategy is impossible to sustain if we view our commitment to self-care as our right and our highest priority. However, it's possible if the prize we're ultimately striving for is found in others' success.

---

2   Walter Mischel, Ebbe B. Ebbesen, and Antonette Raskoff Zeiss, "Cognitive and attentional mechanisms in delay of gratification," *Journal of Personality and Social Psychology* 21, no. 2 (1972): 204–218.

It comes down to our willingness to surrender our personal gratification. To set our desires and agendas aside, to prioritize the happiness of others over our own, to take care of ourselves so we can take better care of others, and to resist the temptation of being driven by praise, money, acknowledgment, or proving our coach wrong.

If you see ten-year-old me, please fill him in.

CUT THE SELFIE

HEAD
WHERE IS YOUR CAMERA POINTED?

In 2010, a twentysomething guy living in New York decided he wanted to photograph ten thousand New Yorkers on the street to create a photographic census of the city's inhabitants. Somewhere along the way, he also started to interview his subjects so that he could include quotes or short stories from their lives next to their portraits that he posted on his blog, aptly called *Humans of New York*. The blog quickly gained popularity and turned into twenty million social media followers; three books; five different photo series that include veterans, refugees, and pediatric cancer patients; and a world-wide audience that gets daily glimpses into the lives of strangers in over twenty different countries.

The name of the guy behind all this is Brandon Stanton. Never heard of him? Exactly.

HEART

BRANDON'S LIFE DRASTICALLY CHANGED BECAUSE HE POINTED THE LENS AWAY FROM HIMSELF.

We've become a society obsessed with ourselves. When you scroll through your social media accounts, do you ever feel like it's one huge contest? Look at what I have, look at what I'm doing, and look how good I look while I'm doing it.

Self-care is not for the purpose of getting; it's for the purpose of giving. When Brandon lost his job and decided to spend the next period of his life think-ing not about money but about how he spent his time, he used his unemployment checks on photography equipment. He did this with the intention of making oth-ers feel seen. To share glimpses of their stories and highlight the undercurrents of life that people aren't always so willing to express. It was to acknowledge that it was their world and he just lived in it.

Why does it matter where your camera is pointed? Because it identifies your motivation and shows what's important to you.

HANDS
TAKE MATTERS INTO YOUR OWN.

- Spend thirty days pointing your camera toward others. That means not only cut the selfie, but don't be in the picture at all. Include a caption that tells an aspect of the story of the person(s) in the photo.

- Check your motives before you post something. How many of your followers will be envious and how many will be inspired?

- If you pray, practice praying for the specific needs of others before you pray for your own.

- Spend thirty days talking—on social media . . . on the phone . . . in person— about *who* you have in your life, not *what* you have. Every time a conversation veers to you, redirect it to a person in your life that you value. Maybe that person is in front of you.

JOIN THE MOVEMENT

Help us celebrate *who* we have, one story at a time.

Follow @RedKeyRevolution for inspiring stories. Hastag #TheRedKey so we can share your story.

REENVISION YOUR BELIEFS

Cut #2: Cut the DIY

I used to spend Saturdays with my grandfather. My mom's dad was the cornerstone of our family, a consistent presence, and some of my fondest memories were sitting in his basement while he taught me life truths from the ever-present Bible he carried around. I was fascinated by him; he'd accomplished so much, yet there was this incongruence—at least on the surface—between who he was in his professional life and who he was at home.

He was a brilliant man who had two honorary PhDs and was the hugely successful president and CEO of a large engineering company. In 1975, he received the Society of Manufacturing Engineers (SME) Gold Medal Award in Detroit, Michigan. Henry Ford II also received an award there. After retiring from W.A. Whitney at age sixty-two, he consulted for many large companies, like Correct Craft and Anderson Industries, but ultimately wanted more time to engage in ministry.

He was often asked to speak at engineering schools like MIT and Purdue, and he would waive his speaking fee if they would let him talk about God. But usually he didn't even ask permission. He'd just start off all his talks by giving his testimony of how God saved him.

Between my mom, dad, and grandfather, I was surrounded by incredible role models who provided me with a very balanced environment: I felt safe but not hindered, supported but not pressured. Even though I grew up in a Christian home— one might call it a Christian bubble—it was never "Believe this because we said so." It was "We'll serve as an example, but we want you to come into your own faith."

The Saturdays with my grandfather occurred around the same time that I received the red key challenge from my youth pastor. Unfortunately, if there was faith in my decision to accept his challenge, it was a very immature faith in God. It was faith in myself and my ability to set, chase, and reach my goals.

Later that year, having stuck with my early morning study sessions, note cards, and multiple read-throughs to grasp subject concepts, I accomplished the first goal on my list: middle school valedictorian. Check. It was the first piece of evidence in my case for self-care. I had now proven that if I wanted it and worked for it, I could have it.

What was interesting is that my parents, while extremely proud, came up to me after hearing the news and said, "You know we love you no matter what grades you get, right? All we ever expect is your best effort." I knew that. But they didn't motivate me to get A grades; I motivated myself to get A grades. I had a deep belief that I could do anything if I set my mind to it. Strong beliefs translated into strong actions, which translated into checked boxes and realized dreams. Some will tell you that's enough—that's the sum of life. I would have.

Has there been a time where belief in yourself trumped rationality or feasibility? What was the outcome?

I started high school and the Jordan Kemper show continued. Then, out of nowhere, my world came to a screeching halt when my grandfather passed away at the age of eighty-seven. I had only known him for seventeen years.

I sat in the front row at his funeral and watched hundreds of people—my grandfather's former employees, families he had supported financially, people who flew in from different countries—show up to pay their respects. There was an open mic where people got to share what he had done in their life. One woman got up and said, "Most of you don't know me, but Harry Conn paid for my son to go to college." My family and I looked at each other like, *Who the heck is that?* Another woman got up and shared how my grandfather had bought her daughter's prom dress because she couldn't afford to. Again, my family had no clue who she was. One person after another spoke about the significance he had made in their lives. He never said a word to any of us about any of it.

Significance is a loaded term. At first it appears like a simple word with a simple meaning, defined as "the quality of being worthy of attention; importance." We use it all the time in daily lexicon to describe things we equate with having worth.

But there's worth and then there's value.

When you think about it, the term *significance* implies some type of recognition, which requires other people. If we were by ourselves with no people around, could we have significance? Not really. We can't bestow the title upon ourselves. True significance is only attained when value has been provided to someone else. Others receive it and others declare it.

So in that way, we can't really find significance—it finds us. We can try to seek it out, but it ultimately can't be attained without someone bestowing it as truth. My grandfather was found significant by all of those people, and it wasn't just that he was found important *by* them; he was important *to* them. It was the first time I realized there was a difference.

I sat there in tears. *My grandfather is in a box and we're all out here reminiscing about the impact he made in our lives. He's gone, and one day that will be me. What sort of legacy am I going to leave behind?* I felt totally lost and completely found.

It was a clear moment between me and God, a realization that I wanted to live a life that meant something to others, just like my grandfather had. He wasn't motivated by money or titles; his life was about the individuals he came across and about the lives he helped change. He set the bar extremely high, and I wanted nothing more than to emulate him—to be important to others by being important to their success. To have people cry and share at my funeral how significant I had been to them. It was my most important goal yet.

Two weeks after my grandfather's funeral, I won homecoming king (check). I wore a pink Hawaiian shirt that used to be his, and as I walked down the football field after getting crowned, I saw my grandmother in the stands with tears streaming down her face. I didn't know whether it was because of the shirt or because she was proud of me, but it solidified my desire for the latter; I was determined to carry his torch. Being deemed popular and important by my peers was a good start.

I graduated later that year as the valedictorian of my high school class (check). I felt like I was acing the placement exam that was my life: By performing at a certain level, I gained acceptance to the next level. My success in middle school determined how I did in high school. How I did in high school would determine which college I'd attend. How I performed in college would determine whether I got into medical school. It wasn't about learning; it was about winning one phase to get to the next phase. Onward and upward, chasing the path.

The path led to college decisions. I had done my due diligence and studied up on my options, visited campuses, and had conversations with basketball coaches at Division I schools. Between my grades and my sports accomplishments, I was offered a few full-ride scholarships. I was elated until my dad sat me down and told me that he and my mom felt really strongly that I should go to a Christian college, so much so that they intended to pay for it. *Are they serious?* I had scholarship offers from top universities, but my dad, who was not a rich man, wanted to pay for me to go to an expensive private school.

Were you an obedient kid? Growing up, I didn't do some of the things I wanted to do because I respected my dad and wanted to honor his authority. Even though I didn't always agree with or understand him, I always obeyed him. He would say, "One day you'll understand," and I somehow mustered enough maturity to trust him in that. My decision about college was no different.

I visited some Christian colleges, and among them was Wheaton. They had a phenomenal basketball program, the coach wanted me to play (check), and their pre-med program was one of the best in the world. *I'll make it work,* I thought.

The first year of college was brutal and among the hardest of my life. I went from a big fish in a small pond in Rockford to a tadpole in an enormous lake at Wheaton. I was a nobody. I became depressed, lost weight, and felt like I lost my identity. If I was a smart kid before, I was now the dumbest person in the world. Surrounded by students with all these high ACT and perfect SAT scores, I felt like I had walked into Hogwarts as the only nonwizard.

My one sanctuary had always been the basketball court. My whole life, I'd walk in and an immediate calm would come over me. Just hand me a ball and I'd know what to do. I was now so unhappy and so homesick and so out of my element that even the basketball court held little refuge. Coach could see it and he benched me. When he did, it was rock bottom.

Actually, what I thought was rock bottom turned out to be a mountain peak, because shortly thereafter, I was bumped down to the JV team. I had been a Division I prospect and was now playing JV at the Division III level. I was ashamed, embarrassed, and broken. I had fallen so far.

Christmas break came, and I was ecstatic that I had not made the travel team because it meant I got to go home for four uninterrupted weeks with my friends and family. I was relieved to be able to take off my armor.

Do you ever feel like the painful times in life are where you grow the most? Pain and adversity—some call it a wilderness phase of life—promote incremental growth that's usually only seen in retrospect. We feel like we're being torn apart, but we're actually just being stretched.

There's a fable about a little boy who found a caterpillar, kept him in a jar, and watched him create a cocoon. He knew the caterpillar was going to go through a metamorphosis and become a butterfly, and he watched every day, waiting for the butterfly to emerge. One day it happened—a small hole appeared in the cocoon and the butterfly started to struggle to come out. The concerned boy decided to help, so he got scissors and snipped the cocoon to make the hole bigger.

As the butterfly came out, the boy was surprised. It had a swollen body and small, shriveled wings. He expected that at any moment the wings would enlarge and expand to support the distended body. But it never happened, and the butterfly spent the rest of his life crawling around swollen, shriveled, and unable to fly.

It turned out the butterfly was supposed to struggle. The butterfly's fight to push its way through the tiny opening of the cocoon pushes the fluid out of its body and into its wings. Without the struggle, the butterfly never properly forms and never develops its ability to fly.

During Christmas break, I got a phone call from my coach saying one of the guys on the team was ineligible. He needed me to come to Washington, DC, for a travel tournament. I was devastated—I would have to cut my break short and head out there the day after Christmas. He sensed my hesitancy.

"You've got a decision to make right now," Coach said. "If you don't do it, you're communicating to me that this basketball program is not important to you and you might as well not play."

I was hesitant for a split second longer and then reminded myself that I committed to playing basketball, and Jordan doesn't quit something he committed to doing. "I'll be there, Coach."

And I was. Barely. Four games, ten points total. Come sophomore year, I rode the bench.

I was as frustrated as I was confused. What was this unfamiliar territory? Hard work had always resulted in me achieving my goals. Personal belief meant I had unwavering confidence. Challenges were fleeting moments to be overcome with tenacity. What was this slump and how could I get myself out of it?

I went into the coach's office and pulled out stat sheets to show him who he had been playing, the minutes they were averaging, the points, and the rebounds. "I can double that," I told him.

"Jordan, I'm really sorry," he said, "but you're a tweener."

TWEENER

noun | informal

1. not big enough to be a forward and not fast
enough to be a guard

Suddenly I was ten years old again and my coach just grabbed my belly fat in front of my teammates. An all-too-familiar feeling of shame came over me, and this time I got pissed off. *You don't know what you just did, Coach.*

They say sports don't build character. They reveal it.

I cleaned up my diet, I amped up my exercise, I kept my head down, I went in early, and I stayed late. When conditioning called for twenty reps, I did thirty. When others slept in, I was up before the sun. I worked so hard that I went to another level. I came back from the off-season in immaculate shape and thought that my junior year was surely going to be my chance to play. It wasn't.

Coach kept telling me, "Jordan, I just don't believe in you."

While he was offensive and brusque, I was forced to recognize that it wasn't that my coach didn't like me or didn't want to win games—he just didn't think I was the solution. He flat-out didn't believe in me. How could I change his belief?

I thought of my grandfather. He famously never balanced his checkbook, never had a sense of how much money was in his bank account. All he knew is that he intentionally lived on far less than he earned so he could give the rest away. If somebody needed money for something legitimate, he'd just write a check and give it to them, and his banker would have to figure it out. That type of person can be referred to as a "hilarious giver"—one who finds so much joy in giving.

At every practice, we played first team (the starters) against second team (me). Hour after hour, day after day, it was a constant reminder that I fell short of the bar. I was discouraged and disappointed, and felt like I had nothing else to give. How was I supposed to rise to the occasion if my coach kept stunting my growth?

Joyfully.

I made a conscious decision to change my attitude. I was among talented, hardworking guys whose potential shouldn't be hindered by a coach-enforced label. I believed in my abilities and I believed in this bench-sitting band of brothers, in what we could do together.

While it's true that belief alone rarely gets us where we want to go, belief usually does determine whether we even try to get there. Oh, how we tried. And you know what? We beat the first team in almost every practice. Coach would get so angry, like he took each loss personally. He kept trying to fix the starters, and the second team kept sitting the bench.

Senior year started, and I was voted team captain by my teammates. Are you surprised that the guy from the bench was named captain? I was too. *This is my time,* I thought. *I'm finally going to start. I'm going to lead this team and we'll win games like Wheaton does.*

The coach always had the list of starters and their match-ups on the board in the locker room before a game. On our first game of the season, I walked in expecting to see my name, but it wasn't on the board. I looked once, twice, three times as if it would appear. It didn't. It almost physically hurt, the disappointment was so heavy. What could I do?

I had nothing left to lose—neither my starting position nor my pride. So, I decided to go for broke and give it my all.

Have you heard of Diana Nyad? She's a long-distance swimmer who attempted to swim from Cuba to Florida five different times over the course of thirty-five years. Except for her first attempt in 1978, she embarked on the 110-mile swim unprotected (without a shark tank), which had never been done before.

Her attempts were marked by gut-wrenching setbacks: currents and winds that pushed her miles off course, paralyzing jellyfish and Portuguese man-of-war stings, dehydration, respiratory distress, lightning storms, hours-long asthma attacks, hypothermia. Her team forced her to end her swims prematurely, and each time was like a punch in the gut; each time the dream was crushed.

Her expedition team was made up of some thirty people. Navigators, managers, boat crew, weather routers, medical staff, and shark experts brimming with innovation and thirst for scientific discovery. But arguably, the most important member of her team was her best friend and head handler, Bonnie.

After her four previous attempts, everybody—scientists, sports scientists, endurance experts, neurologists, her own team—said it was impossible. It just simply couldn't be done. But Bonnie looked at Diana and said, "If you're going to take the journey, I'm going to see you through to the end of it. We'll find a way."

Diana trained for months, both physically and mentally— sports physiology studies have shown that in extreme marathon-type activities, mental determination is a more important factor than physical energy—by swimming between eight and twenty-four hours straight. She knew she'd be left alone with her own thoughts, so she memorized a playlist of eighty-five songs to loop over and over in her head as she swam. She also had counting systems ready in English, German, Spanish, and French to keep her mind sharp.

Prior to her swim, Diana said, "I don't want to be the crazy woman who does it for years and years and years, and tries and fails and tries and fails and tries and fails, but I *can* swim from Cuba to Florida, and I *will* swim from Cuba to Florida."

The day came. Before the first stroke, standing under the Cuban flag waving above, her team was out in their boats, hands in the air, screaming, "We're here! We're here for you!" Bonnie grabbed her by the shoulders and said, "Let's find our way to Florida."

Find a way. Obstacles, heartache, adversity, turmoil. Faith, perseverance, grace, belief.

The team had a cardinal rule that Diana was never to know how far she was, how far she still had left to go. On the third morning, seeing that she was suffering and hanging on by a thread, Bonnie said, "Come here," and waved Diana over close to the boat. "Look, look out there."

She pointed to light.

Diana saw a stream of white light across the horizon and said, "It's going to be morning soon."

Bonnie said, "No, those are the lights of Key West."

Game on.

Fifteen hours later, in August 2013, on her fifth bid at the age of sixty-four, Diana Nyad became the first person to successfully complete the swim from Cuba to Florida. She swam a trip of 113 miles in fifty-three hours.

We are only confined by the walls we build ourselves.

For the first seven games of my senior-year season, I led the team in rebounds . . . off the bench. I made the all-tournament team off the bench. It wasn't until my friend Johnnie had a season-ending knee injury that Coach was forced to start me. Two games later, I scored thirty-eight points and pulled in sixteen rebounds—a school record at the time. I'm still not sure whether Coach's belief in me grew or he was just out of options, but he played me an average of thirty-seven out of forty minutes for the rest of the season. Finally, with the chance to play, I led the entire conference in rebounds. I made all-regional honors and was an all-conference player.

At the end of every season, it was customary for the coach to hand out honors and awards at a team dinner. Since I had led the team in more than one important category, I expected the MVP award to be mine. Nope. It was handed to an underclassman who showed tremendous potential for the program.

I won Most Improved Player. *You were terrible but now you're less terrible* is what I imagined my coach saying as he handed me the award. The word humbling doesn't even begin to describe the moment.

Have you ever been a tweener? In other words, has anyone blatantly expressed their lack of belief in you?

The last time I saw my coach, he said, "Thanks for all you did and thanks for your leadership. What is your honest feedback for me as your coach?"

How much time do you have?

"Coach, it's really hard for me because I can't fault you for your belief systems. Your belief system was that I wasn't good enough, and for that reason, you didn't play me for three years. But I proved to you in my senior year just what I was capable of doing. Imagine if you had given me a chance four years earlier. I feel like you wasted three years of my playing career."

He looked me right in the eyes. "Jordan, I'm sorry. You're right. If I could go back in time, I would have given you a chance."

Did that admission feel good? Sure. Do I often wonder where I'd be if he had believed in me? Definitely.

Here's my point. Human behavior is a product of belief. Belief in ourselves is enough to get us going, but it will never be enough to take us to the peak of our potential. To get there, we need others to share our beliefs as though they were their own. Sometimes we even need others to believe in us more than we believe in ourselves. Every Diana needs a Bonnie. I could've used a Bonnie back then too. But not having one taught me an unforgettable lesson about the power of one person's belief in another.

John Maxwell calls it the ultimate transfer of a leader—when we take the belief that we have in people and pass it on until the people own it for themselves. It's no longer borrowed. It becomes their own belief and it changes them for the better.

When you consider the scope of sacrifices you can make for another person, sharing your belief in them is a small sacrifice that can make an enormous impact.

CUT THE DIY

HEAD

WHAT GREAT ACCOMPLISHMENTS
IN LIFE CAN YOU DO BY YOURSELF?

Professional boxing is known as a solo sport, but Muhammad Ali wouldn't have been successful without his coach, trainer, and nutritionist. Having a baby takes at least two people—not counting the hospital staff—and raising that child takes a village. Getting a promotion takes the boss who agrees to give it to you and, likely, a coworker who helps keep you sane. Being the Super Bowl MVP takes an entire team of players who catch, kick, run, or block. Diana Nyad swam alone in the water but had a crew alongside her with Bonnie at the helm. I was able to lead the entire conference in rebounds only because my teammates played great defense. Nothing great in life ever happens alone. Admit it.

HEART

IT TAKES AS MUCH HUMILITY TO LET OTHERS SERVE YOU AS IT DOES TO SERVE OTHERS.

Have you ever offered to do something for someone—make a meal, throw a party, drive the carpool—and they refused? My wife calls that a "bless block." As in, "Don't block my blessing." There's not much you can do if they don't accept your offering, but it makes you wonder. Do they really not need it or do they just think they would be inconveniencing you? Have you ever been the one who said no to receiving help?

Everyone thought Diana was out of her mind to attempt the swim for a fifth time. She had a fierce self-belief and could have assumed that was enough of a driving force that she didn't need Bonnie's support. But self-belief has a ceiling. The fact that Bonnie chose to believe in Diana, and the fact that Diana graciously accepted Bonnie's help, is the reason she was ultimately successful. You can't control being a Diana—you have no say in whether or not someone chooses to believe in you— but you can choose to be a Bonnie. You can choose to lend your belief to others. And when it's offered to you, you can choose to receive that belief rather than blocking it.

In the DIY world we live in, it can be harder to be a Diana than a Bonnie. But you don't have to pick. Commit to being both.

HANDS
TAKE MATTERS INTO YOUR OWN.

- Acknowledge the next time you can't do something on your own by asking someone for help. Then . . . here's the kicker: Actually let them help you.

- Where are you struggling with self-doubt? Who could you ask to come alongside you? Name that person and reach out. Tell her/him something like this: "To have your belief in me would take me to the next level."

- Now flip it around: Who in your life could use an injection of your belief? Write down his/her name and reach out this week.

DARE TO DIVE DEEPER WITH ME ON THIS CUT?

Free Video at RedKeyRevolution.com/CUTS

RECALIBRATE YOUR GOALS

Cut #3: Cut the Glory

Tell me I'm not the only person who came out of college feeling lost. Thrust onto the precipice of figuring out what to do next meant there were so many options, routes, pressures, and choices. Despite my list of goals and my confidence in achieving them, my balance felt threatened.

I had stayed in college longer than I had originally planned. After graduating with a degree in four years, I decided to go for a second degree and, because of a loophole in the NCAA, was eligible to play another sport for two semesters. So, I joined the football team and proceeded to enjoy college sports for the very first time.

In contrast to my previous coach, my football coach saw my potential and gave me the opportunity to be the best I could be. I loved being on the football team a hundred times more than the basketball team, and not just because my first seven catches were touchdowns. But that helped.

About one hundred guys were on the team, and it didn't matter whether we were the scout team, first team, second team, third team—everybody was important to the cause. The coach was so intentional about building camaraderie and unity among us that he hosted small group meetings once a week and a team-wide chapel on Fridays instead of practice. It promoted deep connectedness. For spring break, we all traveled overseas to places like Honduras, Romania, South Africa, and Senegal to work with alumni serving there.

On those trips, teammates became brothers. Instead of spending a week off school in a sunny location partying with girls, we served alongside one another in humbling and arduous circumstances and developed a bond that was unmatched. Fast-forward to game day: we'd line up on the field next to the brothers we had served with, who we'd been in the trenches with. To have a coach foresee the value those experiences would bring us—not just as individuals but as a collective team—was the greatest gift we never expected.

I was sad to see that phase of my life end, but after six years in college it was time to officially grow up. I graduated from Wheaton for the second time and fell head over heels in love for the first time.

Rachel was my dream girl. I met her early on at Wheaton when I was a freshman and she was a junior, but she didn't give me the time of day. Undeterred, I knew that someday, somehow, I'd find a way to date her. Surely if I set the scenario up correctly, I would do all things right, and she would feel so loved and cherished by Jordan Kemper that it wouldn't be humanly possible to not fall in love with me. She was a trophy to be won and she became my next empty box to check.

Patience won the race, and the next two years were a long-distance courtship, with Rachel in Fayetteville, Arkansas, and me in Chicago.

In the meantime, like many new grads, priority number one was money. My parents were generous enough to pay for my first four years at Wheaton, but the additional time was on me, and student loans don't pay themselves. I also needed money to live so, you name it, I did it. I was a personal trainer and a private basketball coach for kids. I did some accounting services and I worked for my dad on Saturdays, all while studying to take the MCAT. I was headed for the prominent position of physician.

Then I heard about a casting call for people who had recently graduated, were white, and could dunk a basketball. That was me! I went to the audition and got cast in a Converse commercial with Dwayne Wade. All I had to do was show up and dunk, and I'd get paid. The day before the shoot, I got a phone call telling me that Dwayne Wade wanted to use his cousin in my place. The casting director apologized profusely and told me he'd find me another job.

I was more disappointed than I thought I'd be—as much about the money as the feeling of being easily replaced. Furthermore, I wondered, *Had I been bitten by the acting bug?* I thought about penciling it into my fifth-grade list.

A few weeks later, the same casting director sent me on an audition for a football movie called *The Express*. There was major buzz around the multimillion-dollar budget and the fact that Dennis Quaid was the star. I read the lines, was told I was one-dimensional, and didn't get the part. A crushing blow, because how could I be the next Ryan Gosling if I was one-dimensional and couldn't land a role? The feeling of failure that came over me was not a welcome one.

The next day, I enrolled in a Fundamentals of Acting class on my way to audition this time as a stuntman. I was one of thirty-seven former football players who got the job and ended up being the stunt double for the guy who won the role I wanted. I took all the hits, did all the work, and made only a fraction of his paycheck.

Splitting its time between the front and back of my mind was the question of whether or not to pursue my lifelong dream of becoming a doctor. Ever since reading *Gifted Hands* by Dr. Ben Carson in fifth grade, all my academic decisions had hinged around getting into medical school. Before long, I had completed the MCAT and interned for two hundred hours with four different medical groups, but now that it was upon me, I felt torn. Health and the human body undoubtedly interested me, and I wanted to be a big-shot scrub-wearing surgeon and play an instrumental role in people's lives. But there was suddenly lingering doubt about whether becoming a doctor was right for me. The goal I wrote down years before hung over me like a weight. Had I changed my mind or grown up? Or was I just a coward?

During that time, both my roommate and a close friend were drafted into the NFL. *I'm fast and strong and have a great work ethic,* I thought. *There's nothing these guys can do that I can't do. I'll become a professional football player.* An arena football coach encouraged me to get more experience, get more tapes, and build on my two years of college ball. I tried out for a spot on the Bloomington Extreme roster and was offered a contract right then and there.

When someone asked me what I did for a living, I didn't know what to say. Stuntman, actor, football player, personal trainer, potential medical school student, boyfriend, or budding entrepreneur.

I had heard about a nutritional supplement company through a physician from Rockford after my mom experienced some health issues. Dr. Hryszczuk was in the process of leaving his medical practice so he could devote more time to helping people via the company's preventative health and personal care products. The organizational model was built on direct sales, and I caught a glimpse of a new opportunity for me—what if I got involved? I could make good money, I could be my own boss, and it could free me up to pursue avenues that gave me a real platform, like football or acting. I was intrigued.

Soon after, I spent one of my rare days off with Dr. Hryszczuk and filled him in on where life had recently led me—professional sports, the entertainment industry, medical school, and Rachel. He said, "I don't think you're very clear on your vision. You need to figure out what you want."

Really? I hadn't seen it.

His honest assessment hit me like a ton of bricks. He was right. I had my hand in so many things, my focus and energy were so divided, and I was spread so thin. A jack-of-all-trades is a master of none, right?

"Would you rather marry Rachel or be a football star?" he asked pointedly. "Would you rather marry Rachel or be a celebrity in the entertainment world?"

I didn't skip a beat. "I would rather marry Rachel."

That moment held clarity: I loved Rachel, and if I wanted to marry her, I needed to have a responsible occupation and get to a position where I could provide for another person.

But I want to be a famous actor. And a famous football player. And a successful doctor. I'd be able to make an impact from an incredibly large stage. I'd have a platform to speak to people like my grandfather had. I could influence the masses.

Although our lives are different, I'm betting you've been through similar situations where justifications are just a means to escape what you don't want to admit. Somewhere deep down, I knew that the drive behind all those endeavors was the desire for affirmation. I wanted significance and importance. I was chasing recognition in many forms. Sure, it looked like I was on my way to do something *huge*. But I knew the real world inside me.

After the conversation with Dr. Hryszczuk, I was transported back to my grandfather's funeral. *Jordan, it's not about you.*

That same day I canceled my football contract and called my casting agent to tell him no more auditions. I was going to focus on only one thing for one year: building a new business. I thanked God for the motivation that was Rachel.

Six months later, she broke up with me.

A buddy of mine named Andy Studebaker got his high school jersey retired after he made it to the NFL. There was a celebration at the football stadium where he used to play, and that's where I was when I got a phone call from Rachel saying we needed to talk. And then without warning, she just did it. Broke up with me right there over the phone. In disbelief, I fell to the floor like a piece of sludge, shaking.

Andy, who was twice my size, came up behind me and picked me up. It felt like the arms of God. He scooped me up, embraced me, and for one fleeting moment, there was a hint of peace. He told me everything was going to be okay. He told me he was there for me. And when he let go, so did my strength.

I couldn't sleep that night. I tossed and turned and went back and forth between angst and bitterness thinking about how I gave up every single thing, every contract, every opportunity, all for her. I couldn't wrap my brain around it.

Up until that point in my life, I felt like I had controlled nearly everything; everything I put my mind to I accomplished. But now there I was, not able to control the outcome because I couldn't control the other person. I could control every other variable. I could control how much I was willing to work—how hard I worked, how long I studied, how much I read, how far I ran, how high I jumped—that was all on me. But getting another person to do what I wanted them to do? I was powerless. All I could control right then was my reaction to it. My reaction was not good.

When was the first time you realized there was a limit to your influence, a limit to your ability to influence an outcome?

To get through the night, I convinced myself that Rachel was just having a moment. I told myself she would call me in the morning and turn this whole thing around. She didn't. For the next six months, I was just as in love with her as the day she broke up with me. My pain was on par with my freshman year of college; I felt empty, clouded, and alone. *Where do I go from here?* It was defeating, like my road suddenly led to nowhere. I didn't yet know that some paths can't be discovered without first getting lost.

In 1968, chemist Spencer Silver was tasked with inventing a big, strong, tough adhesive. Experiments in his lab resulted in a polymer that was the exact opposite of the goal laid out before him—instead of holding on to objects after it was applied, the polymer let go easily. In other words, he invented the worst glue in the world.

Silver was convinced there could be a good use for his invention and was approached in 1974 by Art Fry, a colleague who had heard him talk about his glue debacle at a seminar. Fry had been at a Wednesday-night church choir practice and had bookmarked his hymnbook with pieces of paper, but by Sunday morning they had all fallen out. He realized the perfect solution would be a bookmark that would stick to the paper without falling off but that wouldn't damage the pages.

Upon hearing Fry's potential solution, Silver was ecstatic. They joined forces and after years of prototypes, tests, technology snafus, marketing hoops, and proof-of-product value, the Post-It note was introduced nationwide in April of 1980. Today, 3M produces fifty billion Post-It notes each year.

Can you imagine if Spencer Silver had scrapped his idea after he fell short of his initial objective? Instead, he maneuvered and kept going and accomplished something different, something even greater. What he failed to accomplish turned out to be the best thing to ever happen, not only to office supply consumers, but also to the 3M Company. In 2010, Silver and Fry were both inducted into the National Inventors Hall of Fame.

It wasn't failure, it was adjustment.

Are you good at adjusting? If you're anything like me, your obsession with goals is so resolute that it's been a detriment to progress and relationships. It's not the actual goal-setting that's dangerous but the unwillingness to accept anything less than complete attainment. Many of my errors, faults, and regrets stemmed from being so committed to achieving my goals, to winning the prize, to being the best, that I would step on or do whatever was necessary to reach it.

Cheating is a sin in my mind—in most people's minds, actually. Nevertheless, I remember organic chemistry being so complicated that I used to bring in notes on test day and put cheat sheets all over the ground. And I justified it in my head. *The point of cheating is to get a good grade, and I need a good grade so I can be a doctor. And being a doctor will help people. So cheating on a test is ultimately about helping people.* Because I couldn't grasp the information and didn't feel as smart as the other students, I cut corners and compromised my values.

The ways in which we achieve goals, as well as the pros and cons of setting them in the first place, can be a double-edged sword. As an enthusiastic and faithful goal-setter, I feel they provide necessary long-term perspective, short-term motivation, focus, and accountability. Motivational speaker and author Stephen Covey touts total commitment to a goal and tells his readers that by starting with a clear destination, they're ensuring their steps are going in the right direction.

But every coin has two sides. Researchers say the downside to goal-setting can include a rise in unethical behavior, a narrow focus, distorted risks, the corrosion of organizational culture, and reduced intrinsic motivation.[3] Perhaps most potentially harmful of all is when goals take over our life and we're willing to sacrifice whatever it takes to attain them—people, ethics, values. Personal gain is a very slippery slope.

Even though I played team sports my entire life, it wasn't really until college football that my motivation to be the best started to shift toward being the best for the sake of my team. Personal gain started to mean collective gain. Think of it this way: If you're getting faster, your team is getting better. If you're getting stronger, your team is getting better. If you're catching better and blocking better, your team is getting better. That shift can be traced back to my football coach and the team culture he provided. He used to say, "I'm not interested in making football players; I'm interested in making men."

Every team has a culture, good or bad. It's the expression of their values, attitudes, and goals about tasks, competition, and relationships. While a good culture doesn't always guarantee success, a bad one nearly guarantees the lack of it. It's a top-down mentality—the coach can influence it, preach about it, and model it, but then it's up to the players; the control of the culture ultimately falls on them.

---

3   Lisa D. Ordóñez, Maurice E. Schweitzer, Adam D. Galinsky, and Max H. Bazerman, *Goals Gone Wild: The Systematic Side Effects of Over-Prescribing Goal Setting*, HBS Working Paper 09-083, (2009).

Media providers tell us plenty of stories about sports divas and their tirades about contract negotiations, playing time, and franchise visibility. It's proof that competition can foster an extremely egocentric culture. Ask any player and most would tell you their goal is to win and/or be the best. But what if to do that, to succeed at winning and being the best, they had to think of others before they thought of themselves?

In his first four seasons, the Golden State Warriors' David Lee started all but two games, was an NBA All-Star, and averaged a double-double. But in his fifth season, largely due to an injury, he had reduced minutes and a new role as a sideline guy. "I see this as an opportunity to prove that I am a team guy, prove how much I care about winning," he said. "All season long, it's sacrificing. Not just me, but other guys, too. That's what it takes to win a championship."

Another Warriors player, Andre Iguodala, went from starting every single game of his career to zero starts after he transferred to play for the Warriors. He referred to his role as, "Always needed, seldom noticed." His acceptance of his role, playing to his role, and trusting his coach earned him the NBA Finals MVP.

In 2015, Tom Brady restructured his contract to give the New England Patriots $24 million in cash to use on other players. He said he'd rather make less money and surround himself with players who get paid what they're actually worth.

Major League Baseball shortstop Cal Ripken Jr. played in 2,632 consecutive games for the Baltimore Orioles. There is no doubt he was less than pumped to play every single game. He experienced illness, fatigue, personal life issues, and injuries, but "The Iron Man" of baseball never let his team down. He didn't want glory; he wanted to always be there for his team.

US Olympic gymnast Kerri Strug destroyed her ankle on her first vault attempt during the women's all-around competition in 1996. Since each gymnast is required to do two vaults, she stepped up to complete the twisting Yurchenko—one of the most difficult moves, but one that has the highest eligible vault scores in women's gymnastics. She received a score of 9.712, which earned the US team its first-ever team gold medal.

Multiple Super Bowl winner Ronnie Lott smashed his pinky finger on his left hand during a play. That offseason, in order to avoid the hassle of surgery and recovery time that would have kept him from helping his team in the 1986 season, he decided to have it amputated.

These athletes modeled what it meant to selflessly serve the team. They put the goals and best interest of the team ahead of their own. Instead of pouting, creating problems within the culture, or quitting, they recalibrated and said with their actions, "I will make your goal my goal." Their at-all-costs mentality was altruistic instead of selfish.

Do you do good for good's sake or to get credit?

There's hope for us all even if our original goals are self-serving. If we can become cognizant of growth and open to flexibility, we'll be better prepared to take advantage of opportunities along the way—opportunities that are right under our nose that might not have existed at the time the goal was set.

During a high school cross country championship in Minnesota, a senior named Danielle LeNoue suddenly fell to the ground a half mile from the finish line of the 2.5-mile race, with what would later be deemed a torn patella tendon and meniscus. She lay there sobbing and in pain as dozens and dozens of competitors raced past her.

But Melanie Bailey, a runner from a rival high school, stopped to help. Danielle encouraged Melanie to keep going to the finish, but she refused. At first Melanie tried to have Danielle lean on her so the two could walk together, but when Danielle was unable to put any pressure on her knee, Melanie picked her up and carried her a half mile on her back across the finish line. They finished 178th and 179th out of 180 runners in the final race of their high school careers.

If you had asked Melanie prior to the race, she would have said her goal was to win.

Then her goal was to finish.

Then her goal was to help Danielle finish.

What if the pursuit of our goals made the goals of others possible? What if your goals could not be achieved apart from others reaching theirs?

CUT THE GLORY

HEAD

WHO'S ON YOUR PEDESTAL?

One of the key elements of Navy SEAL training is Hell Week. It's at the onset of the program and is designed to weed out the weak so that a class of hundreds eventually graduates as a class of dozens. You might think "weak" implies not being able to withstand the sleep deprivation or the extreme mental and physical toughness needed to succeed, and that's correct to a degree. But weeding out the weak also means removing those who see themselves as individuals. In order to be successful, you have to learn how to operate flawlessly as a team. It's never about you. You'll never have to carry a 150-pound log or a 200-pound inflatable raft over your head for hours by yourself, you'll never be sent into combat by yourself, you'll never carry out a mission by yourself, and you'll never be left behind. Individuals fail; teams survive. It's that simple.

HEART

LIGHTING SOMEONE ELSE'S CANDLE WON'T MAKE YOURS ANY LESS BRIGHT.

The title of Navy SEAL undoubtedly entices people. In the minds of many, to be a SEAL is to sit at the apex of human capacity, and to achieve the designation is an extraordinary accomplishment. Many possible motives could drive someone to attempt it, not least of which is the desire to be recognized for doing something that many think is impossible. You're heralded as a hero who lives your life at the outermost boundary, where many would be extremely uncomfortable.

But what's under the mystery, intrigue, and danger? What's beneath the glory? Service. When you cut it all away, it's a band of brothers who risk their lives because they're dedicated to our country and its citizens. They don't refer to themselves as SEALs but as "team guys," and they don't give or take individual credit. They carry their own weight only so they can be strong enough to carry one another.

HANDS

TAKE MATTERS INTO YOUR OWN.

- Who are you helping that you will never get any credit for? Make a list:

_____

_____

_____

- Go through your social media apps and turn off notifications for thirty days.

- What three goals of yours cannot be achieved without giving others the glory? List them:

  _____

  _____

  _____

- Make a list of your most important "thankless" jobs (have you heard it said that your greatest contribution may not be something you do but someone you raise?):

  _____

  _____

  _____

WILL YOU RECALIBRATE YOUR GOALS WITH ME?

Free Video at RedKeyRevolution.com/CUTS

REFOCUS YOUR EXPERTISE

Cut #4: Cut the Preaching

Rachel got married eighteen months after she broke up with me, and I proceeded to not go on a single date for five years. You can imagine that left a lot of time for work.

Throughout my early twenties, I dedicated my time to my nutrition business, but I still had bouts of thinking that maybe I'd go back to playing football or become an actor and prove to Rachel and everybody else that I could do it if I wanted to. Some days I felt like I was standing on the life version of the Four Corners, and I just wanted to keep straddling those states. I didn't want to plant my flag in any one location. On those days I'd ask myself, *What would my grandfather do?* Almost as though he were next to me, I could hear him say, "I would figure out a way to help people. I would stay committed to that cause. You've built up your business and brought other people into it, so you owe it to them to stick it out. They've been through painful experiences just like you and they keep going."

When the business opportunity fell into my lap post-college, it aligned perfectly with what I was looking for in a job. I knew I wasn't willing to go into a situation where somebody else controlled what I could and couldn't do. I wasn't willing to work for someone like my basketball coach, who wouldn't affirm me or give me opportunities to succeed. I prided myself on outworking every other human being, and if I was going to work harder than everybody else, I needed to be compensated for it. I wanted an opportunity where my financial future was up to me.

Because of the way this particular supplement company was structured, building success through direct sales and recruiting new customers, I knew that it would turn out to be whatever I made it. If it didn't work, it was my fault. If it did work, it was my fault. Challenge accepted.

When I was growing up, I occasionally helped my dad at work. One time he was building a new house, and he brought me with him to help with the subfloors. We swept away the dirt and dust so we could prep for the new hardwood to be installed. Not surprisingly, the subfloor was covered with drywall compound—like putty that had turned to cement. The dried adhesive had stuck to the subfloor due to the carelessness of the installation crew.

Most builders don't get too picky about removing it because they're just going to put new flooring over it, and as long as there aren't big mounds sticking up, it doesn't pose a problem. But under my dad's direction, I labored away on the subfloors and scraped off gunk for two days.

"Why do we need to scrape this mess off when we're just going to put new floors over the top of them? Nobody will see this," I said to my dad.

My dad didn't miss a beat. "The owners will never see the subfloors, but we'll always know they're there. If we're going to do something, we're going to do it well."

As years went by and more and more people joined my business, I felt the pressure of responsibility; their livelihoods were, in a sense, in my hands. It was an authoritative feeling, like when you're asked to babysit a kid that's only one year younger than you. They seemed to trust my judgment and advice. They appreciated my training and perspective. They were trying to better themselves and looked to me for help. I liked being at the helm of the ship.

I had found my sweet spot. I worked long hours and didn't feel it; I didn't care if people called me in the middle of the night; I didn't care if I had to get up before dawn every day of the week to put something together for somebody I was training or leading. I loved the grind and felt important.

In the midst of all this, the curveball known as *The Bachelorette* was thrown into my life when the senior casting producer asked me to be on the show. I was flattered and intrigued.

I talked to my dad about it, and he said, "Jordan, I don't question your heart, I don't question your conduct. But good conduct in a strip club isn't good conduct at all."

But Dad, I'm going to be the next Tim Tebow. I'm going to go on TV and show people how to properly treat a woman. People love the virgin who doesn't drink.

I came up with every justification for why I should be on it, and they all stemmed from what Jordan wanted—significance and importance.

I said yes to the show.

Immediately I felt off. I wanted to do it, but I wanted even more to have peace again. I called the producer back and told them no, please cancel my flights. What good would have come from it? I was frustrated with myself that I got stuck in the trap of wanting to be number one, be the star of the show, be in the spotlight . . . again.

Back to work. I could at least get that right.

At twenty-five years old, I became the fourth-fastest grower at my company. I had climbed the ranks as this young kid from out of nowhere and rose at a pace it normally took someone ten to fifteen years to accomplish. I built a successful home-based business as a young person, and the powers that be wanted to put me on stage at a speaking engagement with Dr. Oz, a trusted sponsorship partner of the company, and four other physicians. And so there I was, onstage in front of three thousand people, alongside five doctors practicing an occupation I had aspired to attain for so long. The year following that first speech, I spoke to over one hundred thousand people in thirty different cities across the globe.

Malcolm Gladwell says it takes roughly ten thousand hours of practice to achieve mastery in a field. The logic is that in order to do a craft well, it takes a significant amount of deliberate practice. To come to that conclusion, he studied the lives of extremely successful people to find out how they achieved success.

In 1960, an unknown high school rock band named the Beatles went to Hamburg, Germany, to play in the local clubs. They were underpaid, the acoustics were terrible, and the audiences were unappreciative. So what did the Beatles get out of the Hamburg experience? Hours of playing time. Nonstop hours of playing together that forced them to get better.

As the Beatles grew in skill, audiences demanded more performances, which meant more playing time. By 1962, they were playing eight hours per night, seven nights per week. By 1964, the year they burst onto the international scene, the Beatles had played over 1,200 concerts together. By way of comparison, most bands today don't play 1,200 times in their entire career.

And then there's Microsoft. Bill Gates and his friend Paul Allen dropped out of Harvard to form the company in 1975. What at first appears ridiculous and irresponsible makes a bit more sense when we learn that Gates and Allen had thousands of hours of programming practice prior to founding Microsoft.

They met at an elite private school that had raised $3,000 to purchase a computer terminal for the school's computer club in 1968. A computer terminal at a university was rare in 1968, and Gates had access to one in eighth grade. The boys took to programming like moths to a flame.

The Gates family lived near the University of Washington. As a teenager, Gates would sneak out of his parents' home after bedtime to use the university's computer. Gates and Allen easily acquired ten thousand hours of practice, and when the time came to launch Microsoft in 1975, the two were ready.

One fascinating point of the Gladwell research—no "naturally gifted" performers emerged. If natural talent had played a role, they would have expected some of the "naturals" to float to the top of the elite level with fewer practice hours than everyone else. But the data showed otherwise. The psychologists found a direct statistical relationship between hours of practice and achievement. No shortcuts. No naturals. Underdogs unite.

I may not have quite reached ten thousand hours as I practiced mastering the art of public speaking, but if expertise could be measured in joy, I was an expert. You know those times when you can tell people are really paying attention to what you have to say? Or you see them putting into practice something you mentioned? I saw people react positively to my guidance and it made me feel good, like I was slowly earning the right to lead people.

Do you remember the feeling of wonder when you mastered a skill for the first time? Could you get it back by becoming a student again?

Most high earners in my organization had contracts requiring them to be paid a fee by event organizers to speak, but I just asked the organizers to pay for my expenses. I was making a very successful living—at times it felt like more than I deserved—but at the end of the day, money wasn't a driving force for me. Wouldn't you think that someone who always wanted to be the best, someone who grew up having the *me-me-me* attitude down to a science, would also want the fanciest house, nicest car, and most expensive suit? But money had never been my motivation. Maybe it goes back to my grandfather and seeing all those people at his funeral, knowing the legacy and impact he left; he gave all his money away. His dollars were merely certificates to help people.

When the recession hit, my dad's business struggled. The economy had tanked and few people were building homes. My dad was resourceful and optimistic, though I could tell he was also anxious, and I felt guilty because I knew he would have been in much better financial shape if he hadn't paid for me to go to Wheaton. It became important to me to pay him back, and I also wanted to be prepared to take care of him and my mom if that was ever needed.

A lot of people who joined my business either wanted to improve their health or their finances. When their primary focus was their income, I would see them making decisions based on that motivation. They would push someone into the business who wasn't ready, or they would upsell someone and convince them to spend more than they could afford. But when their main focus was physical wellness, they were solution oriented and would support someone in whatever way was best to help them attain optimal health. Could they be motivated by both? Sure. But one always inched its way to the front.

If I asked you what Zappos's expertise was, would you say shoes? You'd be wrong. Their expertise is their customer service, and I don't just mean free shipping and no-hassle returns. They're experts in personal connection.

The company handbook has only one rule: "Be yourself and use your best judgment."

They have five hundred employees who work at their call center in Las Vegas, and all of them went through seven weeks of training. As an example of their workload, in just one random day in May 2017, they received 7,394 calls and answered them in an average of twenty-five seconds.[4] Agents don't use scripts and never respond with "That's against our policy" or "Let me get a supervisor"—instead, they customize solutions for each different customer. They make sure the caller hangs up thinking *This company wants to be my friend.* On the wall of their office is a chalkboard with hand-drawn stats around how many flowers, cookies, postcards, and unnamed "wow gifts" have been sent to customers in the previous month and previous year.

A prime example was when a customer called trying to return some boots. It turned out she had bought them for her father, who had since died. The Zappos customer service rep told her not to bother returning them; they would refund her money and she was free to give the boots away instead of sending them back. After the call, the rep sent her some flowers. Some time after that, she sent the rep a letter and a photo of her father.

The rep later said, "The flowers weren't what mattered. The *phone* was. It lets us have these in-depth, textured conversations with our customers. It's the key to how we build customers for life."

From the get-go, Zappos knew that the people behind the purchases were what was most important to them. They practiced what they preached and mastered it. They're successful in

---

4   Micah Solomon, "Tony Hsieh Reveals The Secret to Zappos' Customer Service Success In One Word," *Forbes* (June 12, 2017), https://www.forbes. com/sites/micahsolomon/2017/06/12/tony-hsieh-spills-the-beans-the-one -word-secret-of-zappos-customer-service-success/#570aba3a1acc.

large part because they consciously and continually put people before profit.

There's so much to learn from that business model, not least of which is that listening is the greatest compliment you can give another person and the most profitable form of investment in their lives. John Maxwell, an author, speaker, and pastor, says every time he meets with someone, he heads into the meeting armed with a list of questions he knows he wants to ask. He wants to make the most of the time he has with them, but he also wants to engage with them and show he values them by getting to know them. Doing so requires that he ask questions—they talk, and he listens.

The common form of listening is for our own sake, to get an edge, to make our point, to offer our advice. But the greatest power of listening lies in listening to learn the needs and desires of others. Author Stephen Covey says, "Most people do not listen with the intent to understand; they listen with the intent to reply."

Are you a story-topper? It's one of my weaknesses. I used to chomp at the bit when waiting to interject with my own thoughts or tales or experiences while in conversations with people. I was a total one-upper and would find myself talking right over people. *Do you really think the guy at the gas station cares about your forty-yard dash time in college, Jordan?*

After several years in business, I slowly learned what it meant to be attentive. I found myself calling every new person just to introduce myself to them and get to know their story. Some weeks I made over one hundred calls. I would ask about their "why" and their intention for joining so I could really understand and empathize with their situation. Who knew that hearing was a physical ability, but listening was a skill?

Think about people who have pulled the best out of you— what did they ask? How well did they listen? Did your opinion matter?

To learn anything—especially as an adult—is humbling, because it's a blatant acknowledgment that we don't know something, that we have something to learn. Many years after my post-college minor life crisis, I saw that being worried and stressed and confused about which path to take in life had been a normal reaction. Obviously, we controlling overachievers hate when we don't know where we're going. It started to click for me that maybe we aren't called to figure everything out but are instead called to be good stewards of what we are given.

After a stellar college football career as a linebacker at Arizona State University, Pat Tillman was drafted by the Arizona Cardinals in 1998. Even though he was comparatively shorter than others who played his position, he outplayed them all. He loved the game and played the next few years as a safety for Arizona, even turning down a five-year, $9 million contract offer from the St. Louis Rams out of loyalty to the Cardinals.

In May 2002, eight months after the September 11 attacks and after completing the fifteen remaining games of the 2001 season that followed the attacks, Tillman turned down a contract offer of $3.6 million over three years from the Cardinals in order to enlist in the US Army.

Pat and his brother Kevin, who walked away from a professional baseball career with the Cleveland Indians to enlist, completed basic training, the Ranger Indoctrination

Program, and Ranger School together before being deployed to Afghanistan. Pat was killed in action in April 2004 at twenty-seven years old.

Controversy surrounded his death after it became known that he was killed by friendly fire; initial reports had stated that it had been at the hands of the enemy. But here's what's not controversial: To play at the highest level of competitive sport takes supreme skill and a commitment that few have. To give that up—to change professions, embark on a completely new path, and become totally competent in another field—took guts. He had a deep-rooted conviction and a warrior's heart. He refocused his expertise because he felt called to use his abilities elsewhere.

Conventional wisdom would tell us that in order to become world-class, we should only focus on one field. Put in our ten thousand hours, master it, and call it a day. But what if we're called to more than that?

The word *polymath* comes from a Greek term meaning "having learned much" and describes a person whose expertise spans a significant number of different subject areas. It's often associated with great thinkers of the Renaissance and the Enlightenment who excelled at several fields in science and the arts, like Leonardo da Vinci, who was a painter and anatomist (among other things). The term proved just as applicable throughout later generations—Thomas Jefferson was an inventor and politician, Vladimir Nabokov was a novelist and entomologist, Howard Hughes was an aviator and filmmaker.

History is full of iconic achievers who attained the pinnacle of human potential, and we applaud them for their profound commitment to greatness. They're whom society looks to when we need proof that we can exceed limits and do a great many things.

But what if our fields of expertise went beyond occupational parameters? What if we spent ten thousand hours learning to be kind or mastering the art of resilience or perfecting how to be empathetic? We can look to iconic servant-leaders who sacrificed their own aspirations for the sake of others—people like Mother Teresa, Nelson Mandela, and Albert Schweitzer—and admire them for the profound impact they had on humanity. What they teach us is not only inspiring, it is life- and career-altering for those who embrace it.

When my parents took me to Wheaton for my first year at college, we found that my dorm room had super-tiny desks. My dad knew I liked to spread out when I studied, and he knew the tiny desk would drive me nuts. He looked at the specs of the room, then measured the current desk and determined it had twelve square feet of total desk space. He went out and bought lumber and crafted a desk that went over the original desk and quadrupled my space, all because he wanted me to have room to create and work.

What if the best part of having an expertise is getting to use it to improve the lives of others?

CUT THE PREACHING

HEAD

WHAT IF WHAT YOU SAID MEANT NOTHING?

"Do as I say, not as I do." We've all heard it and we've all said it. Which is unfortunate, because it's hypocrisy at its finest. Imagine what a powerful experiment it would be if the only instruction others could follow were based on your actions instead of your words. If you couldn't speak, you would be held accountable for your actions without the accompaniment of explanation. If no talking were allowed, you would be judged solely on how you carried yourself. If words were off-limits, your love, respect, and admiration could only be expressed through service. Who you are would come down to what you do. To lead a life of significance, you would have no choice but to lead by example.

HEART

BEING A GREAT SPEAKER ISN'T AS IMPORTANT AS BEING A CURATOR OF GREAT CONVERSATION.

Effective Leadership 101: ask great questions. People don't care what you know; people care what you want to know about them. Dale Carnegie goes as far as to say, "Remember that a person's name is to that person the sweetest and most important sound in any language." It's not about feeding their ego; it's about showing them you respect them enough to inquire.

How much closer would you pay attention if you knew you had to commit something to memory? There's a difference between listening when someone speaks and being able to comprehend enough of what they're saying to retain it. You have to engage at a much higher level in order to sufficiently absorb the content. That's listening with true intentionality—imagine if that were the set of ears we all chose to listen with.

HANDS

TAKE MATTERS INTO YOUR OWN.

- Instead of telling others what to do, show them by your actions. If it makes sense, do it with them.

- Ask people questions that require more than a yes-or-no answer.

- Some examples:
  - What's the most important issue you're dealing with right now?
  - What roadblocks are holding you back?
  - What can I do to make you more effective?

- Instead of being focused on catching people doing something wrong, turn your attention to catching people doing right. Be a student of others so you can compliment them on something positive you noticed. Are they generous? Instead of saying, "You're generous," you could say, "Hey, I really noticed the way you served that person."

- Instead of actively speaking—aka only listening to others' cadence in order

to know when you can speak again—
practice active listening, as if you
have to repeat their responses back
to them.

PAUSE FOR A SECOND.
TAKE A DEEP BREATH.

Just know that I'm proud of you.

Significance is not something that you learn in one book. It's the revolution happening in your soul—a shift of your heart and mind. We are all at that intersection between who we are, who we were, and who we want to become. Embrace these cuts, and you will unlock a lifetime of impact.

Now let's jump into my favorite chapter . . .
you're about to meet my wife!

REALLOCATE YOUR GROWTH

CUT #5: Cut the Quick Fix

In 2012, British researchers conducted a study where they asked participants to cycle as hard as they could on a stationary bike for four thousand meters. "Really go for it, push yourself," they were told. The goal was to cycle the distance in the shortest amount of time possible. The results of their performance were used as a baseline.

Later, the participants were given the same instructions—cycle four thousand meters as hard as you can—but this time they raced against themselves. Using 3D software, a computer-generated avatar that represented their baseline performance was displayed on a large projector next to them. Could they beat their original race time, even though they had already given it everything they had?

What the participants didn't know was that the avatar was actually going faster than their previous ride. The results?

Every single cyclist surpassed their avatar's speed and rode significantly faster than their previous maximal effort.

If we continually compete against others, we become bitter. If we continually compete against ourselves, we become better.

If you played competitive sports then you know you have to be quick to forget your wins and your losses. In football, whether we won or lost, there was always another game next Saturday. In golf, whether or not you play well on the third hole, you have to forget about it and move on to the fourth hole. Move toward the next week, the next game, the next hole. Capitalizing on momentum means we keep the ball rolling. It could be bad breakups, rank advancements, flat tires, big paychecks, missed deadlines, or lucrative partnerships, but the important thing is to keep forging ahead.

I had a coach who always used to point his crooked finger at us and say, "You gotta keep on walking. There's gonna be dips and there's gonna be hills, but you've got to be like a bulldozer and stay even-keeled, and no matter what comes your way, you just keep on walking."

Fast-forward to a college basketball game where we played the number one team in the nation. At halftime, we were down fifteen points and totally in our heads about it. I gave that speech to my team and even pointed my finger for full effect. I hadn't played a good first half, so the pep talk was as much for me as it was for them. When we huddled up and broke, it was an acknowledgment that our despair from the first half could not and would not keep us from moving forward.

We came out and absolutely dominated the second half. I hit five three-point shots in the first four minutes and had twenty-five total points. With three starting freshmen and two guys hurt, we caught up, took the lead, and beat the top-ranked team in the nation. The place erupted. It wouldn't have happened if we'd sat in our disappointment.

Lasse Virén was a twenty-three-year-old police officer when he made his Olympic debut in 1972. His first event was the ten-thousand-meter race. In the twelfth lap of the race, Virén was in fifth place when he suddenly stumbled and fell. He rose quickly—as if it were pure reflex to jump up and run—and kept going. Now significantly behind, in less than 150 meters he caught up with the leading pack. Then, with 1.5 laps to go, Virén applied pressure. One by one, his opponents fell behind. He won by six meters and broke the world record. It was one of four gold medals he'd win in his career.

When is the last time you fell? How long did it keep you down?

We win by meters, lose by seconds, gain by inches, fail by miles. Metrics are important. When we measure our goals, we track our progress, and when we track our progress, we improve our results. Bench press, measurements. BMI, measurements. Income, measurements. If we're not somehow growing, we're dying. It's good stewardship to be focused on progressing forward, but it always comes back to the why. Tony Robbins says, "Change is never a matter of ability; it's always a matter of motivation." What's behind your movement?

In my line of work, I'm around people who are striving to be as optimally healthy as possible. They're trying to lose weight, eat right, and stay active. However, it's not necessarily the regimen that's difficult but the motivation necessary to

THE RED KEY REVOLUTION

make those good choices and follow the plan. I've always said that the two most motivated groups of people I work with are athletes and pregnant women.

Athletes are so regimented because there's often a tangible consequence—a winning record, a trophy, a contract. And pregnant women—well, because of what's at stake, expectant mothers are beyond disciplined. What they cut out, what they add in, how they treat their body. They put that child first because the motivation of another person's life is so strong. It's the purest pursuit. Making intentional choices for someone before they're in our lives is one of the most profound ways to honor them.

From carrying a child to raising a child, mothers and fathers have sacrificial jobs that are motivated by the love they have for their children. The lengths parents go to is proof that pain is a stronger motivator than pleasure. They will go to the ends of the earth to ensure the child doesn't go through the pain of not having their basic needs met or the pain of not feeling accepted. Just think about parents in third-world countries who walk miles back and forth every day for water. It's not to quench the child's thirst; it's to ensure their child's survival.

In 1962, a boy named Rick Hoyt was born as a spastic quadriplegic with cerebral palsy, and doctors told his parents that the brain damage was so severe he would never be able to participate in mainstream society. The doctors recommended he be institutionalized since he was going to be in a vegetative state for the rest of his life.

Rick's parents, Dick and Judy, didn't listen. Instead, they decided to raise him like any other child. Though Rick couldn't

speak or use his arms or legs, they knew he was paying attention because they'd see his eyes follow them around the room.
His mother spent hours trying to teach him the alphabet with
sandpaper letters, and then posted signs on every object in the
house. His parents took him camping, sledding, and swimming.
They fought to integrate him into the public school system,
pushing administrators to see beyond his physical limitations.
At the age of eleven, they arranged to fit Rick with an inter-
active computer. With this computer, Rick could form words
by highlighting letters of the alphabet with a tap of his head
against a headpiece. It was with that communication device
that he was permitted to attend public school for the first time.

In middle school, Rick heard about a student who had
been in an accident and was paralyzed from the waist down. A
charity road race was in the works to help the student pay his
medical bills. Rick came home and told his dad, "I have to do
something for him. I want to let him know that life can go on
even though he's paralyzed. I want to run in the race."

At the time, his dad was forty years old and definitely not a
runner. But Dick saw how amped up his son was, and he knew
he had to do something. They headed out to the five-mile race
and he pushed Rick in his wheelchair. They finished all five
miles and came in next to last. When they got home that night,
Rick wrote on his computer, "Dad, when I'm running, it feels
like my disability disappears."

Team Hoyt was born.

Dick started training. He ran every day with a bag of
cement in a wheelchair to simulate Rick's weight. He engaged
in resistance exercises, weight training, and bicycling, and

maintained a strict diet of whole foods and low fat. He took swimming lessons because he had never learned to swim. Their mantra became "Yes you can."

Over the next thirty-nine years, the father-and-son team completed 1,130 events: 72 marathons (including 32 Boston Marathons), 257 triathlons (including 6 Ironman and 7 Half Ironman), and 97 half marathons. For the swimming stage of triathlons, Dick pulled Rick in a boat with a bungee cord attached to a vest around his waist. For the biking stage, Rick rode in the front of a specially designed tandem bike. For the run portion, Rick rode in a custom-made racing chair (like an adult-sized jog stroller) that his dad rolled in front of him. Each time they crossed a finish line, Rick raised his right arm into the air in victory.

The disabled boy that was deemed "nothing but a vegetable" graduated from Boston University with a degree in special education in 1993. His first racing chair went on display in the Sports Museum of New England in 1994. He got to carry the Olympic torch through Boston in 1996. He was inducted into the Ironman Hall of Fame in Hawaii in 2008.

Throughout the course of their journey, Dick had a heart attack and three stents implanted. He had severe carpal tunnel syndrome from pushing his son's chair through three decades of races. He had a torn meniscus, a ripped hamstring, and multiple surgeries. His dedication to his son put him on the verge of bankruptcy and contributed to the collapse of his thirty-year marriage.

"I'm not a hero," he once said. "I'm just a father. And all I did was tie on a pair of running shoes and push my son in his wheelchair. It's like I'm his arms and legs, but he's the one running. I have no desire to do this on my own. He drives me."

At some point, the pain of not doing something becomes greater than the pain of doing it. It's the essence of motivation. What pain are you willing to endure?

In my late teens, I dated a girl and the relationship started moving forward physically. I kissed her a couple times, and then one night we had a conversation about our stance on physical purity and what it meant. I told her that waiting until marriage was very important to me, but she expressed that it's only natural that two people in a relationship who are attracted to each other are going to move forward physically; it's undeniable.

I thought about the commitment I made at thirteen years old in front of my pastor and peers, the symbol of purity that still lived in a drawer in my room, and how much it now meant to me to honor it. By then I understood.

"I'm really sorry, but I have to disagree with you," I said. "This is a decision. A decision we can make right now. I'm raising my hand to say that nothing is going to happen physically between the two of us, and it's going to be really difficult if only one of us is fighting that fight. We need to both be on the same page."

"I think it's really self-righteous of you to think you could overcome this," she said, her tone steeped in judgment.

How would you have taken that? Was I being accused of self-righteousness because I thought I could remain pure? Suddenly I'm the bad guy for trying to stand up for what's good, for what's important to me? I thought she'd be excited or impressed with my stance on purity, but instead she was mad at me.

"I'm really sorry, but I can tell that we're not on the same page. I have a red key I'm not willing to give up. I think this has to end tonight."

She didn't know about the red key. She looked at me, puzzled, and then got angry, then sad, then said something about never dating again. Then she turned and left. I stood there alone feeling like a terrible schmuck.

No one said this would be easy; I was only promised that it would be worth it.

An ongoing expression in my family growing up was "Fear God, not man." We were taught that every decision we made needed to come from the right spirit and from the right attitude of heart. We should stick to our convictions and do what we felt was right; our job was not to answer to man's expectations but to God's.

That mindset can help eliminate our need to be people pleasers, but it can go too far if taken in a direction of blatant disregard or self-righteousness. It's safe to say that the first twenty years of my life were spent not caring what other people thought because doing so would have interfered with reaching my goals. If considering their opinions, thoughts or needs wasn't imperative to what I was trying to accomplish, then it wasn't in my best interest. At least that's how I framed it in my mind. My hypocrisy was that I actually cared deeply what people thought of my efforts and successes. When I felt they didn't see me and what I had to offer—like my basketball coach—I got angry. Fortunately, I had people around me, particularly in my family, who understood how to legitimately not "fear man."

With the correct intention behind it, being unconcerned with what people think can be the healthiest of boundaries. When we know it's not them we ultimately answer to, it frees us to go after what we feel called to do; public opinion doesn't prohibit us from acting on our greater purpose.

Despite feeling like a schmuck, my moral compass was telling me to keep moving in the direction of purity. Fear God, not (wo)man. I stuck to the courage of my conviction and stayed motivated by the promise of what was to come.

And ten years later, it paid off.

I kept coming across this girl on social media. We had some mutual friends, and I started following her on Twitter. I tweeted at her and she never responded. I followed her on Instagram and friended her on Facebook. The more I watched her, the more impressed I got, and my awareness of her continued to increase over the next six months. She was beautiful and, based on what she was posting, we shared similar values. *If she's the real deal, I'm going to find a way to meet this girl.*

After a few unanswered Facebook messages, she finally responded. Brief. Casual. We had months of sporadic back-and-forth communications until she eventually gave me her phone number. She was shocked when I called her since no one seemed to speak on the phone anymore. "So, what's your story?" I asked within the first minute. We became friends and started to find little pockets of time to connect.

She had planned two mission-type trips to Haiti and Uganda following her college graduation and communicated on her pages that she was looking for financial support. If you've done similar trips, you know the sacrifice it takes to make that trek and do that work. *This girl is no joke.* I hopped online and anonymously donated to her trip. The amount I gave was based on math—10 percent of my latest paycheck as was my custom. Unbeknownst to me, that amount was the precise amount she lacked, down to the penny. Her full payment was due the next day. She woke up and clicked the link to see if any more money had come in overnight, and she discovered she had every dime. I can't take credit for that. I consider those details a God thing.

Kristen went to Haiti, and when she returned I told her I had clients in the Tampa area and asked if I could fly out to meet her. *She won't think I'm crazy if I make it a work trip.* She gave me a two-day window. I flew from Chicago to Tampa, scared out of my mind, and had no idea what to expect.

Picture your most awkward first date. In another state. We spent the next forty-eight hours among her friends and family, getting to know each other in that blundering, nervous way. Over meals, outings, and conversations, I definitely felt that she kept me at arm's length. I left thinking that I'd like to see her again, but I didn't know if the feeling was mutual.

Several weeks later she was going to be in Seattle on business. *My sister lives there and I've been meaning to visit.* I asked if she'd like to meet up, and when she agreed, I hurriedly booked my ticket and made arrangements.

We had a nice time together—certainly more comfortable and easy than when we were in Tampa. We spent time with my sister and her family, went sightseeing, and took care of our different business responsibilities. Over dinner on the third night of our trip, we really focused on getting to know each other; we took our conversation to a depth that surprised us both. We talked about our pasts, our families, and our motivation for continuous growth. She said she was in constant pursuit to redeem what was broken. I felt as if my soul was looking in a mirror.

The conversation shifted to sexual purity—totally normal dinner conversation—and I told her about my red key. I had never fully unpacked the meaning and significance of the red key to a girl before. Kristen was floored.

I left Seattle having learned that vulnerability was more powerful than invincibility.

We saw each other again before she went to Uganda, and she kissed me before she left. I was taken aback. I hadn't kissed a girl in seven years. *She likes me.* My heart flew out of my chest. *She wants the relationship to move forward.* We officially began dating once she returned.

Several months later, I was asked to do a monthlong speaking tour to Australia, New Zealand, Philippines, and Mexico. I knew that traveling together was a great way to get to know each other—the good, the bad, the ugly—so I asked the parent company if they would allow me to bring Kristen along and if they would pay for her to have a separate hotel room in each city. That was a tall order and something they'd probably never heard before, but they agreed.

We were extremely intentional during our entire dating process. We flew back and forth about every two weeks to see each other. We read multiple books about relationships, engagement, and marriage and discussed the chapters as we finished them. We committed to having an "open-hand stance" with our relationship—we weren't set on any outcome and we were open to "us" not being what was best. Fortunately, we never came to that conclusion.

Eight months after we started dating, I flew out to her dad's house to ask him if I could have Kristen's hand in marriage. As I sat across from him and shared the story of my red key, his eyes filled with tears as he processed what I'd given up in anticipation of one day meeting and marrying his daughter.

When it came to the proposal, I wanted to make sure Kristen felt loved and honored and surrounded by her favorite things. I surprised her by chartering a helicopter that took us to multiple locations. First, we flew to a lake where I asked her if I could have the privilege of being her husband. At sunset, the helicopter took us to a private estate where our friends and family had flown in from all over the country to celebrate with us.

We got married six months later. On our wedding day, before the ceremony, I sent Kristen a sealed letter. Inside the envelope was my red key.

I waited thirty-one years to find my wife. I spent thirty-one years growing into the person she needed me to be. I dedicated thirty-one years to honoring a promise I made. And after thirty-one years, it took me only one second of looking into Kristen's eyes at that altar to realize that it had never been about me at all. It hadn't been about my goal or checking another box; that red key was never my prize to win. It had been about her and the gift she deserved to receive. My deepest joy was seeing the joy on her face that day.

The basic need and desire of every single human being is to love and be loved. That's how we were designed; that's our purpose. And love requires sacrifice. It requires that we hold their interests above our own, that we find gratification in their wins, that we grow strong so we can shoulder their load, that we give up something precious in order to gain something better. It requires that we make decisions on their behalf before we even know who they are.

CUT THE QUICK FIX

HEAD

WHAT SACRIFICE ARE YOU WILLING TO ENDURE LONG TERM?

If you were to decide that you want to get in better shape, you would increase your gym time. You would start slow and work up to more intense workouts with more frequency. You would cut out certain foods and introduce others, track your progress through weigh-ins and measurements, and give yourself pep talks when you inevitably get sick of the gym, leg curls, and egg whites. You would do all this because you know that hard work is hard work.

Or would you use a guest pass at the gym for four hours in one day and be upset afterward when you didn't see an immediate difference?

Our society's progressive mentality of "get it done and get it done now" is at odds with the patience we need to attain things that don't come easily, naturally, or quickly. You get out what you put in, and the harder it is, the sweeter the victory. Commit to the things you desire for the long haul.

HEART

QUIT LIVING LIKE NO ONE IS COUNTING ON YOU.

Every time one of my friends announces they're going to have a baby, they seem to miraculously grow up overnight. If they were already mature and responsible, then they up their game. They immediately look at their priorities, assess where they are and what they're doing when away from their homes, and determine whether it's worth it. They review their finances, start to cut frivolities, and open a college savings account. They become CPR certified and crash test dummy the heck out of the new car seat.

The role of caretaker is an honorable role to have. Anytime someone is reliant on you—in business, in love, in family—it's a powerful motivator and can provide a profound sense of purpose. No one wants to feel like they're letting anybody down. But what if what drove you wasn't just fear of letting other people down but also fear of letting yourself down?

HANDS
TAKE MATTERS INTO YOUR OWN.

- What is a red key cut you can make in your own life right now? In other words, what is worth pursuing and what sacrifice is necessary to get there?

- What cannot get done without a long-term commitment? What must you embrace daily? What must you avoid? Who are the beneficiaries of the commitment besides yourself?

- What are the long-term goals of three people in your life? Now what can you embrace daily to help them get there? What can you choose to avoid?

IF YOU WANT MORE. . .

I challenge you to re-evaluate your goals and assess how you are focusing your ambition, time, energy and unique talent.

Free Video at RedKeyRevolution.com/CUTS

REFRAME YOUR LEADERSHIP

Cut #6: Cut the Spotlight

Back in college, our football team got together on Tuesdays and Fridays during the offseason to work out and run line drills. When we came up even two inches short of the line, the coach would yell, "Hey listen, if you cheat on the line, you're gonna cheat on your wife."

Jarring, right? But it was his way of telling us that we were making small compromises in the habits we were creating. If we couldn't be held accountable to get ourselves two inches farther to the line, we would be just as willing to compromise in other areas of our life.

Coach held us to a standard and urged us to reach our full potential—and he created the environment in which we could do so. The elements that surrounded us not only encouraged our growth but actively developed it. Think about grass or flowers. When conditions are right—warmer temperatures, longer days, more sunlight—they thrive and grow, but when there's inadequate moisture or freezing temperatures, growth gets delayed. John Maxwell calls it the Law of Environment, and its basis is that we grow the most when we surround ourselves with people and opportunities conducive to our development.

In a 1955 study called the Orphanage Preschool Project,[5] children between the ages of one and five years old who lived together in an orphanage in Davenport, Iowa, were separated during the day to attend two different preschools: one the same crowded and unstimulating preschool that had been on-site for years and one newly built preschool with floor-to-ceiling windows, large outdoor play areas, and expert teaching. Both had the same curriculum.

Over three years, researchers observed the children in these two separate environments to track their intelligence, vocabulary, language achievements, and social competence. The results showed noticeably better mental development, verbal expression, social maturity, motor skills, and subsequent intellectual growth among the children in the new preschool. The differences between the two groups were thought to have been caused by the better environment offered in the new setting.

Did your mom ever tell you that you are the company you keep? Your companions are a key part of your environment. Jim Rohn famously said that we are the average of the five people we spend the most time with. It relates to the law of averages, which is the theory that the result of any given

---

5   H. M. Skeels, R. Updegraff, B. L. Wellman, and Williams, H. M., *University of Iowa studies: Studies in child welfare: Vol. 15. A study of environmental stimulation: An orphanage preschool project* (Iowa City: University of Iowa, 1938).

situation will be the average of all outcomes. We're greatly influenced—whether we like it or not—by those closest to us. They rub off on us and affect our way of thinking, our self-esteem, and our decisions. Have you ever found yourself stooping down to someone's level? Then you know why it's important to choose your five wisely.

Author Jim Collins says it's all about getting the right people on the bus. In college football, if we wanted to win more games, we had to have the right people on the bus. If you want to see success in your personal endeavors, you have to have the right people on the bus. Our buses need to be filled with people we're proud to associate with and who make us better—they bring up our average. And it's easier to find those people when we emit admirable qualities ourselves. Who we are is what we'll attract.

Who is on your bus and why?

The home-based business I started when I was twenty-two years old grew into a big organization. As I started to work with dozens, then hundreds, then thousands of people, I thought intentionally about who I wanted to attract and what type of leader I wanted to be. We've all naturally learned from and then taken something from anyone who has ever led us, haven't we? Teachers, coaches, parents, bosses. The law of averages. I began to deliberately think about my ripple effect.

In my years of public speaking, there have been many times when people came up to me afterward and told me how something I said or did resonated with them. I've gotten the same response in situations on a much smaller scale—after conversations at a family gathering or during a check-in with a team member. I've felt the exact same way about others. I'll talk with someone, and a comment they make will stick with me. Or they'll perform a seemingly mundane act—follow through on what they said they'd do, remain positive in a negative situation—and it will serve as a catalyst in making that moment of my life better. A favorite memory of mine was in Montreal, Quebec. I happened to mention my grandfather, Harry Conn, from the stage. Someone in the audience who had heard my grandfather speak found me afterward. He told me that he had seen me many times on stage, and I had always reminded him of Harry, but he had had no clue that I was his grandson until that day. He went on to share that my grandfather was the reason he knew Jesus. Tears filled my eyes, as I hadn't received a better compliment in my life.

Before Game 3 of the 2003 NBA Western Conference quarterfinals, thirteen-year-old Natalie Gilbert, who had won the opportunity to sing "The Star-Spangled Banner" through a contest, took to half-court. She forgot the words moments into the song. Maurice Cheeks, the former point guard for the Philadelphia 76ers, and who was now the assistant coach for the Oklahoma City Thunder, walked over to her. He put his arm around her shoulder, raised the mic to her mouth, and helped her remember the words by picking up where she left off. They finished singing the song together, along with twenty thousand fans.

What if the concept of leadership has been turned into something bigger than us, something beyond us? We've made it about changing the world. It's true that leaders are at the forefront of powerful movements. They perform monumental feats and achieve remarkable results that are recounted in every history book. But what if we've spent so much time celebrating amazing things that hardly anyone can do, that we've convinced ourselves those are the only things worth celebrating?

Think about the characteristics that come to mind when you hear the word "leader." Strength? Fortitude? Persuasiveness? The "It" factor? Many of us who feel called to lead have to work at honing certain characteristics because we're under the assumption that leadership is not a trait we're born with but a skill we build. Recent scientific discoveries confirm the theory that deep intentional practice creates[6] a substance in our brain called myelin, which some neurologists call the holy grail of acquiring new skills. Myelin is a neural insulator that wraps around our nerve fibers and increases the speed at which impulses are conducted—like signals traveling through circuits.

Author Daniel Coyle argues that human ability, whether to play baseball or play Mozart or lead a team, develops when chains of nerve fibers repeatedly carry tiny electrical impulses. When we practice doing something the right way, swinging a bat or playing a note or speaking to an audience, our myelin system responds by wrapping layers of insulation around the relevant neural circuits, each layer adding a bit more skill and speed and memory. The thicker the myelin gets, the better it insulates, and the faster and surer our thoughts and movements become.

---

6   Daniel Coyle, *The Talent Code: Greatness Isn't Born. It's Grown. Here's How* (New York: Bantam, 2009).

Leaders aren't born, they're made. And they're made one incremental step and one intentional choice at a time.

When Air Florida Flight 90 crashed into a frozen lake in the middle of a snowstorm, all but six passengers were killed. Some twenty minutes later, a helicopter arrived to rescue the survivors. After getting one man to safety, the helicopter threw a life ring to Arland Williams, who immediately gave it to the passenger next to him. When the helicopter came back for a third time, he did the same thing again. And again. When the helicopter came back a final time, Arland was dead. He'd used his last ounce of strength to save complete strangers.

During the 2011 Japanese tsunami, Takeshi Miura and Miki Endo were two government risk-management workers tasked with warning and directing the public to safety. When the ten-meter tall wave hit, both Takeshi and Miki stuck to their posts and kept broadcasting, using their last words to direct townsfolk to safety.

Lee Jong-rak is a pastor in South Korea who created a "baby box." He attached the box to the side of his house to provide a safe place for unwanted babies to be dropped off instead of being abandoned on the side of the road. Since 2009, more than 630 babies have been saved and many have been adopted.

Do you think any of those people thought of themselves as leaders? Sometimes we consider the title of leader as something we might deserve one day; but to give it to ourselves right now requires a level of arrogance or presumption that we're not comfortable with. It gives us an excuse to not expect it every day, from ourselves or from each other.

When we choose to lead ourselves through wise decisions and actions each day, we set ourselves up to succeed at the endeavors before us, we create more opportunities than the average person, and we also become a more potent asset to others. Challenge accepted.

Roman emperor Marcus Aurelius wrote in one of his essays that "we came into the world for the sake of one another." Leadership is devoting yourself completely to something that changes people's lives. It's the epitome of selflessness and is not for the faint of heart. Weakness, on the other hand, takes the path of least resistance; as humans, that means being selfish—wanting all the credit and none of the blame. Real strength is measured by what we enable others to accomplish as a result of our service to them, not by the pressure of our grip or the weight of our demands. Attempting to demonstrate just how strong our powers of authority are is the quickest path to confirming our weakness.

Not all leaders are larger than life.

David, a teenager, triumphed over battle-tested Goliath with a sling and a stone. He didn't back away from the chance to do something valiant just because he didn't fit the mold of a typical hero. The odds were stacked against him, but he was courageous in his belief and committed to securing the fate of his people.

The world has never seen a great leader who lacked commitment. Nelson Mandela was a great leader because he saw the vision of his people and was committed to a life of helping them accomplish their goal of freedom. During his twenty-seven-year imprisonment for trying to overthrow the pro-apartheid government, he rejected at least three conditional offers of release. He demonstrated resilience and forgiveness and an unwavering focus on unity, all against incredible odds. After his release, he became the first president of South Africa to be elected in a fully representative democratic election.

But I'll bet you've never heard of the equally committed person named Zelda La Grange, who spent nineteen years working as Mandela's personal assistant once he was out of prison. It was a twenty-four-hour-a-day job that left no time for her to have a family of her own, appropriately foster relationships, or hold social plans.

"It's not only about being a PA, it's about being a backbone to someone . . . even if putting on the kettle will make his life better. I was quite content with serving him, because I could see how much my commitment meant to him and he inspired loyalty."

For the past ten years, I've kept a journal with an ongoing list of people I'm praying for. It helps me track where they are in life, what they need, what they want to accomplish, and how I can best serve them. I devote the beginning of each day to lifting them up. It doesn't always have to be prayer; I encourage those who don't pray to keep a list of gratitude or a list of people to serve or check in with. It's about being thankful and mindful and focusing on how we can support the people around us, even if it's not in a boisterous, outward-facing way.

Are you aware of what the people around you are struggling with? Is it because you don't ask, or they don't tell?

If I told you that it's better to give than receive, you'd likely tell me that's not the first time you've heard that. But have you heard that giving activates the same parts of the brain that are stimulated by food and sex? Experiments show evidence that altruism is hardwired in the brain—it's pleasurable. And there's no shortage of scientific research to prove that giving is a powerful pathway to personal growth and lasting happiness.

A 2008 study[7] found that giving money to someone else lifted participants' happiness more than spending it on themselves (despite participants' prediction that spending on themselves would make them happier). The work included a national survey in which 632 American men and women were asked how much they made annually; how much they spent each month on bills, expenses, and gifts for themselves; and what they spent monthly on gifts for other people and donations to charities. They also asked them to rate their level of happiness.

The findings showed that those who reported spending more on others, what the team called "prosocial" spending, also reported a greater level of happiness, while how much they spent on themselves had no impact on happiness.

In a second experiment, researchers handed envelopes of money to students on a college campus. The recipients were told they should spend the money (either five dollars or twenty

---

7   Elizabeth W. Dunn, Lara B. Aknin, and Michael I. Norton, "Prosocial Spending and Happiness: Using Money to Benefit Others Pays Off," *Current Directions in Psychological Science* (forthcoming). Electronic document, https://dash.harvard.edu/handle/1/11189976 and https://www.researchgate.net/profile/Lara_Aknin/publication/5494996_Spending_Money_on_Others_Promotes_Happiness/links/0c960536bc4c368a69000000/Spending-Money-on-Others-Promotes-Happiness.pdf.

dollars) by the end of that day either on themselves—to cover a bill or expense or get themselves a gift—or on others by buying a gift for someone or making a donation to charity.

The results mirrored the earlier survey. The people who spent the money on themselves weren't happier that evening, but people who spent it on others were. The amount of money, five dollars or twenty dollars, didn't matter at all. The rise in happiness was dependent on how people spent it.

Giving is certainly not limited to money. Spending time volunteering and actively serving others improves the health and well-being of those who do it. Studies show both the physical and psychological benefits that individuals experience when they consistently volunteer their time to help others—like lower rates of depression, greater functional ability, decreased stress levels, and a heightened sense of purpose.[8]

There were six times during and after college when I traveled to Africa with football teams, and each time made our own needs seem even smaller than the time before. We held babies with AIDS, who had no mother and no father and who had never smiled because they'd never felt love; our job was to hold them so they didn't cry. We fixed sewer lines and stood knee-deep in human waste just so the toilet would flush. We built playgrounds and read stories to kids before they went to bed. I would return home and inevitably fall back into the cycle of daily life and evolving responsibilities. And that's when I

8   Francesca Borgonovi, "Doing well by doing good. The relationship between formal volunteering and self-reported health and happiness," *Social Science and Medicine* 66, no. 11 (2008): 2321–2334, doi: 10.1016/j.socscimed.2008.01.011.

knew it was time to set up a service day. The greatest gift we could give ourselves could never be as great as the gift of helping another person. It's as hard a thing to remember as it is easy to forget.

A great Tom Hanks movie quote is, "It's supposed to be hard. If it wasn't hard, everyone would do it. The hard is what makes it great."

All things worthwhile are an uphill battle. Almost everything that has value, almost everything that has purpose, requires work on our part to attain it. We have to put in the effort to get where we want to go. When you rode your bike as a kid, wasn't it fun to go down a hill? It was fast and exciting and you didn't have to pedal. But in order to go down that hill, you had to pedal your way to the top. The thrill only came after the work. Today we live in a culture where people have uphill dreams and downhill habits.

It's not the work that's hard but the discipline. Think about all your daily obligations and deadlines and tasks, all your daily distractions. And then think about how those are doubled, tripled, quadrupled depending on the people counting on you. The price we pay to accomplish it all is usually our time and energy, which can dissipate quickly. How can we fit it all in and still maintain a semblance of sanity? My football coach used to say, "Be a man of routine." Find a rhythm and stick to it. Own your time and own your schedule.

Every Sunday night is spent scheduling out my week. I listen to some music, have my favorite drink, and schedule every activity for each day of the week. Every day there's a morning routine. Every day there's a time set aside to invest in family. Every day there's a midday prayer. Every day there are set check-ins with my team. Every day there's a quick nap time. I get more done in three hours than most people get done in ten because I choose to create a powerful schedule. I choose to do the right things that allow me to control my time and control my mind. The old saying is true: if you fail to plan, you plan to fail.

Plan your workouts, meals, study times, date nights, and when you'll sleep, and then stick to the schedule. That's intentional living. Our thinking creates our attitudes, which create our results, which ultimately create our life. Setting a schedule won't make you more successful—but following it will.

Will it go awry? Will the unexpected occur? Of course. But the foundation is there and keeps the building from crumbling. I've found that the more I am in control of my time, the better my business does, the better my body feels, the more money I make, and the better I can serve others.

Being disciplined helps put our decision-making on auto-pilot by giving our goals a time and a place to live. It makes it more likely that we'll follow through regardless of our will-power levels—when those are depleted, we're more likely to make decisions based on the environment around us.

A six-month study[9] took place in a hospital cafeteria where researchers changed the choice architecture of the drinks. Bot-tled water was added to the three main refrigerators originally

---

9   A. N. Thorndike, L. Sonnenberg, J. Riis, S. Barraclough, and D. E. Levy, "A 2-phase labeling and choice architecture intervention to improve healthy food and beverage choices," *American Journal of Public Health* 102, no. 4 (April 2012): 584, https://www.ncbi.nlm.nih.gov/pubmed/22390518.

filled only with sodas, and water was also added to baskets throughout the room.

Over the next three months, the number of soda sales dropped by 11.4 percent. Meanwhile, bottled water sales increased by 25.8 percent. Similar adjustments and results were made with food options. Nobody said a word to the visitors who ate at the cafeteria. The researchers simply changed the environment and people naturally adjusted the decisions they made. It's studies like this that showcase just how important our environment can be for guiding behavior and achieving success.

We should create environments that make it easy to do the right things and hard to do the wrong things. I have a black binder full of CDs with seminars and sermons and speakers that I listen to. Instead of watching them online and risking distraction by surfing the web and getting lost in social media or YouTube, I burn CDs with the audio versions. I listen to them over and over, and then circulate the binder to multiple leaders on my team. When you're surrounded by better choices, it's a lot easier to make good ones. But the true test of leadership is when we're in an unfavorable environment, and we're tasked with rising above.

In 1942, Desmond Doss joined the United States Army following the attack on Pearl Harbor. He told his parents he was willing to risk his life on the front lines in order to preserve freedom, but there was one catch: he refused to kill an enemy soldier or carry a weapon into combat because of his personal beliefs as a Seventh-day Adventist. When he was assigned to an infantry rifle company, his refusal caused a lot of trouble among his fellow soldiers. They viewed him with disdain and ostracized and bullied him.

His commanding officers wanted to get rid of him; they saw him as a liability and believed that a soldier without a gun wasn't worthwhile. They tried to intimidate him, scold him, assign him extra-tough duties, and declare him mentally unfit for the Army, and they even attempted to court-martial him for refusing the direct order of carrying a weapon. But they failed to toss him out, and he refused to leave.

Desmond never held a grudge. He became an Army combat medic, and things began turning around when the men discovered that the quiet, unassuming medic was the first to appear at their side when a cry rang out on the battlefield. He never considered his own safety and repeatedly ran into the heat of battle to treat a fallen comrade and carry him back to safety.

The men in Desmond's division were repeatedly trying to capture an imposing rock face called Hacksaw Ridge. A small victory came after American troops secured the top of the cliff, but the troops were stunned when enemy forces suddenly rushed them in a vicious counterattack. Officers ordered an immediate retreat. Soldiers rushed to climb back down the steep cliff. All the soldiers except one.

Fewer than one-third of the men made it back down. The rest lay wounded, scattered across enemy soil, abandoned, and dying. Desmond disobeyed orders and charged back into the firefight to rescue as many of his men as he could. His determination and courage resulted in seventy-five lives saved that day.

Desmond Doss did not kill a single enemy soldier during his three years of service. He was an ordinary man who acted extraordinarily, and in turn became a leader among his peers. He went on to receive a Medal of Honor, a Bronze Star for valor, a Purple Heart, the Asiatic-Pacific Campaign Medal with three Bronze Stars, the Good Conduct Medal, the American Campaign Medal, and a Presidential Unit Citation.

Author Marianne Williamson said, "Our deepest fear is not that we are inadequate. Our deepest fear is that we are powerful beyond measure. It is our light, not our darkness, that frightens us." We need to get over our fear of how extraordinarily powerful we can be in the life of another. Only then can we start to value the full impact our actions can have.

CUT THE SPOTLIGHT

HEAD

WHO ARE YOU WHEN NO ONE'S WATCHING?

Think about all the different faces you have. At any given moment, people could see your brave face, straight face, long face, silly face, red face, or bold face. You can choose how others see you by choosing how to project yourself when you're in front of them. But when you're by yourself, when the lights aren't on you and you don't need to be anything but exactly who you are, what face do you wear? Are you proud of what's under the mask or do you need to make some new cuts?

HEART

PEOPLE WHO SHINE FROM WITHIN DON'T NEED THE SPOTLIGHT.

Have you ever been to live theater? You sit in the audience watching the actors on stage, and when they end a scene there's a blackout. When the lights come back up, there's a different environment with new sets and backdrops and props; it's a seamless transition that's pretty baffling considering you don't see anyone making the changes. Bravo to the crew. They wear head-to-toe black, and their job hinges on going stealthily undetected.

But if you dig deeper, you learn about the stage manager. They're in charge of the crew and orchestrate the whole production by calling out every light cue, sound cue, set change, curtain pull, and countless other technicalities that effectively create the illusion of the world you've enjoyed for two hours.

The audience never thinks about the stage manager because they're never seen, heard, mentioned, or applauded. They are the crux of the production and sit in a dark control room night after night, happily never taking a bow. It's a beautiful picture of what it takes behind the scenes to live a life of significance.

HANDS

TAKE MATTERS INTO YOUR OWN.

- Think about the layers that make up who you are. How can you be more transparent with people? What do you need to give up? What must you welcome in?

- What's more important to you, attention or competence? Make sure you're making the right cut.

- Who are the people behind the scenes that make your life easier? Make a list of those you appreciate and praise them publicly.

WANT MORE PEOPLE
TO FOLLOW YOU?

You must re-frame your leadership.

Free Video at RedKeyRevolution.com/CUTS

REDEFINE YOUR LEGACY

Cut #7: Cut the Now

Would you agree that Monday is the most dreaded day of the week? Nine-to-fivers who drive into work on the first day after the weekend know full well what awaits them: all the emails and meetings, not to mention the tasks left over from Friday that they told themselves they'd get to on Monday. The universal acknowledgment of general disdain even spawned the popular catchphrase "case of the Mondays."

Would you be surprised to hear that Sundays are actually the most dreaded day of the week? Sunday at 4:13 p.m., to be exact.[10] Because that's when people's anxiety about the

---

10 Monster.com, "Red, White and Mostly Blue: Monster Data Shows that the US Continues to Suffer the Most from Sunday Night Blues," (June 2015), https://www.monster.com/about/a/Red-White-and-Mostly-Blue-Monster-Data-Shows-that-the-US-Continues-to-Suffer-the-Most-from-Sunday-Night-Blues?WT.mc_n=SM_PR_blog.

work week starts. That phenomenon is referred to as "Sunday Night Blues."

The most stressful day of my week has always been Friday. My business is based on bulk product sales, and 40–50 percent is moved at the end of the work week. Fridays are my head-down, hour-after-hour, rally-cap, scheduled-to-the-minute, hardest working day.

But I don't dread it. As the old saying goes, "If you do what you love, you'll never work a day in your life." It seems I'm in the minority since it was recently reported[11] that 70 percent of Americans either hate their jobs or are completely disengaged. It's a testament to the number of people still searching for their *thing*. Have you found yours?

Chick-fil-A founder Truett Cathy said that the three biggest decisions we make in life are master, mission, and mate. Who do we serve? What is our purpose? Who will we share it with? If life is a matter of choices, then every choice we make makes us. Every single thing we pursue has a consequence, an end result that impacts others as much as it impacts us.

I want the people who work with me to be in the 30 percent. While I can't force them to be content in their jobs or convince them that they pursued the right choices, I can recognize and encourage them on a regular basis. I can purposefully not cramp their style or limit their abilities. I can foster chemistry and camaraderie off the field, since that's just as important as assembling a set of skilled players on it. In other words, I can

---

11   Gallup, "State of the American Workplace," (2017), http://news.gallup.com/reports/199961/state-american-workplace-report-2017.aspx.

do all the things I loved about my football coach and avoid all the things that hurt me about my basketball coach.

There's a difference between leading others to make them happy and leading others to make them better. Understanding the difference means grasping the distinction between happiness and joy. Happiness is like an ocean that ebbs and flows and tends to be reliant on external factors—people, things, thoughts, events. Joy is a state of mind that's cultivated internally; it's foundational to our true being, and every other state or emotion can rest on top of it.

A study on happiness[12] found that acquiring money, education, a big house, or an expensive car does not affect happiness levels as much as we would like or might expect. Many different types of researchers have studied those who win the lottery and have found that, year after year, people who have won are no happier than those who did not have that experience. That phenomenon is called hedonistic adaptation and suggests that everyone has a baseline level of the happiness emotion that they revert back to after receiving something external or materialistic in nature.

Alternatively, Harvard conducted a study[13] over the course of eighty years in which they followed 268 men in the hopes of revealing clues about how to lead healthy and happy lives. They

---

12 Daniel Kahneman and Angus Deaton, "High income improves evaluation of life but not emotional well-being," *Proceedings of the National Academy of Sciences of the United States of America* 107 (2010): 16489–16493.

13 The Harvard Adult Development Study (ongoing), http://www.adultdevelopmentstudy.org/.

found experiencing joy, especially in relationships, made the men feel more protected against life's disappointments, helped to delay mental and physical decline, and was a better predictor of a long and happy life than social class, IQ, or even genes.

Happiness and joy are mistaken for each other all the time. Also on the similar-yet-different spectrum is the distinction between résumé virtues and eulogy virtues. Author David Brooks says it's like we're all walking around with two selves: one self who craves success and builds a résumé full of skills, accolades, and achievements, and a second self who seeks the values that make for a great eulogy—like connection, community, and love. One self wants us to ambitiously build ourselves up, and the other wants us to not only do good, but to be good. One comes with diminishing returns and the other with elevated longevity.

Some pursue impact, but others actually create it.

When we pursue something, we seek it, work toward it, strive for it. To actually achieve it takes clarity of focus. Wise choices are as much about what we do as what we don't do. Apple says that they say no to dozens of good product ideas every day so that their focus can remain on a few great ones. Steve Jobs said, "You have to pick carefully. I'm actually as proud of the things we haven't done as the things I have done. Innovation is saying no to a thousand things."

If focus is used as a noun, it means having a single goal. It's a static thing, a thing you *have*. We pursue a single objective without getting distracted along the way and allow momentum to build as different people rally behind the goal.

If focus is used as a verb, it's not something we *have* but something we *do*. This type of focus is not static; it's an intense, dynamic, ongoing, iterative process. It's Art Fry going back and forth with Spencer Silver until the right idea takes the air out of the room. It's the constant exploration needed to see what the "noun focus" should be.

Imagine if the moment you woke up this morning, your eyes focused one time and then never adjusted again. You would be out of focus all day. Our eyes produce clarity through a perpetual process of adjustment. It's not enough to have; we must do. Focusing on what is essential means developing and valuing both types of focus.

Focusing on the right things in the right way—meaning what we're trying to accomplish and how we're attempting to do it—will bring us a type of success that can't be measured.

Success, in the minds of most, is a personal achievement. They deem something important and they work toward it. When they achieve it, they've succeeded. It can be in a lot of different arenas. In business, success often means wealth. In sports, it's often a winning record. In countless other fields, it could be attaining a certain position, rank, or recognition. Success can be defined and achieved a million different ways, and there are endless perspectives on how to do both:

John Wooden: "Success is peace of mind attained only through self-satisfaction in knowing you made the effort to do the best of which you're capable."

Woody Allen: "Eighty percent of success is showing up."

Maya Angelou: "Success is liking yourself, liking what you do, and liking how you do it."

(Attributed to) Alexander Graham Bell: "Before anything else, preparation is the key to success."

Joan Rivers: "I succeeded by saying what everyone else was thinking."

Deepak Chopra: "Success comes when people act together; failure tends to happen alone."

Michelle Obama: "Success isn't about how much money you make; it's about the difference you make in people's lives."

Melinda Gates: "If you are successful, it is because somewhere, sometime, someone gave you a life or an idea that started you in the right direction. Remember also that you are indebted to life until you help some less fortunate person, just as you were helped."

One of the most important tensions we all face in our quest for success is the struggle between caring well for ourselves and caring well for others. Is it possible to simultaneously embrace our highest aspirations while maximizing our impact?

If we're being honest, most of us spend our lives waking up and thinking about meeting our own needs. It's often not until our needs are reasonably met and we don't have any major distress that we finally give a concerted effort to chasing the needs of others. Once we've found ourselves, or achieved something, or made ourselves valuable, then we have something to give to others.

That concept is not completely out of left field. If we're financially successful, we have more money to give away. If we're retired after a long career, we finally have spare time to devote to others. If we've already checked some main items off our bucket list, we have the predilection to help others achieve the items on their list. There has to be a certain amount of success in our lives before we're willing to take the step toward significance, before we ask ourselves, "What else is there in life beyond professional and monetary success?"

Just as success must be defined before it can be achieved, so must significance. To say something is significant is to say it's worthy of attention. The word itself elicits a high level of importance; it is something you can differentiate from the commonplace. It's distinguished and rare. What's significant is the most important part.

Let's face it, the vast majority of the pursuit of significance comes on the heels of success. When we talk about significance, living a significant life, making a difference, we're not really talking about livelihoods. We're talking about what we hope to accomplish in our pursuit of success. We hope, in other words, that our successes add up to a significant impact on others.

Most people chase success, and when they achieve it, they feel significant. But what if we consciously decided to reverse it? What if we didn't rely on our success to lead to significance but instead chased significance to find success? It took almost two decades after my grandfather's death for me to realize that he was not significant because he was successful. He sought to be significant in others' lives, and that brought his great success.

Significance brings about an attitude of sacrificing your own personal success or your personal gratification for the sake of someone else; it is giving up what you want so that someone else might gain what they want or need.

David Nelson was an NFL receiver for the Buffalo Bills and, later, the New York Jets. After a trip to Haiti in the off-season of 2012 following Hurricane Sandy, Nelson and his brothers started i'mME, a nonprofit organization aimed at ending the Haitian orphan cycle. He made numerous trips back to Haiti and used his influence and platform to grow the organization's impact immensely, leading to the development of housing facilities, educational programs, and job creation. "I played my heart out on the field and lived with the Haitians in the offseason," Nelson said. "I was whole."

Two years later he was released from his contract over concerns that his focus on his organization took precedence over his commitment to the sport. Nelson released a statement: "If given an ultimatum, I choose i'mME . . . but I ask this: What if it were possible to do both, and more importantly, do both really well? If that were the case, what would locker rooms look like? What would this world look like?"

Married Boston couple Jeff Kaufman and Julia Wise make a combined income of over $200,000 a year, yet they live on only 6 percent of it, so they can give the rest to charity. "We don't see what we do as extreme. It's become the norm and we hope [our daughter] also sees helping other people as a part of life."

Harris Rosen is a self-made millionaire who adopted a Florida neighborhood called Tangelo Park. By offering free preschool for children in the community and funding university and college educations for all high school graduates, he cut the crime rate in half and increased the high school graduation rate from 25 to 100 percent.

Warren Buffett and Bill and Melinda Gates started a campaign called The Giving Pledge that encourages wealthy people to contribute a majority of their wealth over their lifetime to philanthropic causes. Membership comes with just two requirements: be worth a billion dollars and be willing to give half of it away.

There are currently 158 signers who have collectively pledged half a trillion dollars. Buffett says, "Incremental wealth, adding to the wealth they have now has no real utility to them. But that wealth has incredible utility to other people. It can educate children, it can vaccinate children. It can do all kinds of things." He also says that most of the members intend to give away a lot more than half. That's certainly true of the founders. The Gateses have committed to giving 95 percent of their wealth away, and Warren Buffett has pledged 99 percent.

Significance is certainly not tied to giving money away, but it is tied to generosity that uses what we have—resources, experience, time, talent, money, expertise—for the pure benefit of others. Key word: pure. Are you solely seeking to have fun, fame, fortune, and recognition, or are you seeking to serve and benefit others with what you have while expecting nothing in return?

Many people think if they do enough and have enough, even if they're self-centered, it will bring fulfillment. But the problem is that self-centeredness and fulfillment cannot peacefully coexist; they're incompatible. When we're too fixated on helping ourselves, we can't properly help others. If only I had understood that at an earlier age.

Out of every goal I set and every goal I reached, only one ended up carrying true significance. None of my radical commitments to personal growth, and no pinnacle of personal achievement that came as a result, matched the success

I earned through my commitment to the original red key. I made a decision and stuck to it—some would call that tough or impressive or commendable—but that paled in comparison to the gravity of what it meant for Kristen. I underestimated its power when I made the decision, but it manifested its power on our wedding day. It was then that I understood that purity was what I sought in every pursuit I had had in my life.

Purity goes well beyond abstinence. It is the freedom from anything that muddies your impact, and involves active choices we make every day in every area of life. That said, the irony isn't lost on me that my purest pursuit ended up being the pursuit of purity. What began as a spiritual conviction that most consider archaic, turned into a decisive illustration of the way I wanted to live my life.

Can you imagine what would happen if we pursued purity in all things?

Tony Robbins says that every human being has six fundamental needs, and all behavior is simply an attempt to satisfy those needs: certainty, variety, significance, love, growth, and contribution. If all our needs are inherently the same, then what makes us truly different is how we go about meeting them.

I always thought if I worked hard enough or my sacrifice was great enough, I would accomplish my goals; I'd be triumphant and win the prize. They were self-serving goals using self-serving antics to attain self-serving success, and therein was the source of my inability to live a life of true significance, like my grandfather did.

I still fall short. It's an ongoing and earnest pursuit. Every night, I look myself in the mirror, stare deep into the pupils of my eyes, and ask myself, "Do you have any regrets from today?" I think about my conversations, how I treated my wife, whether I spent enough time praying, whether the people I worked with felt valued, whether I led with a pure heart, and whether I made those around me happy or better. After thinking through the rhythm of my day, if I have regrets, it keeps me awake at night. But if the answer is no, I sleep like a baby.

Starting the day and night with reflection makes us more conscientious of the wake behind us—the effect we have on all the people counting on us and on those we have yet to meet. We've got to work on ourselves and get ourselves together—not for ourselves but for the people we impact and for the people *they* impact. We could be the first link in a chain reaction.

A woman in the drive-thru at a Starbucks in St. Petersburg, Florida, paid for her iced coffee as well as the caramel macchiato that the customer behind her ordered. For the next eleven hours, 378 people in line continuously did the exact same thing and paid for the customer behind them.[14]

A customer at a pizzeria in Philadelphia told the owner to keep the change and let it pay for a slice of pizza for someone who needed it. The owner grabbed a Post-It note, wrote up a makeshift pizza voucher, and stuck it to the wall in case a customer came in who needed a warm meal and couldn't afford it. One slice turned into hundreds, which turned into thousands,

---

14   Paulina Firozi, "378 people 'pay it forward' at Starbucks," *USA Today*, August 21, 2014, https://www.usatoday.com/story/news/nation-now/2014/08/21/378-people-pay-it-forward-at-fla-starbucks/14380109/.

and now Post-Its line the walls of the pizzeria. To date, the restaurant has given away more than ten thousand slices of pizza, feeding some forty homeless people every day.[15]

A man heard from the desk clerk at his yoga studio that she had recently donated a kidney to an ailing friend. The man was so captivated that he called his local community hospital to ask how he might do the same thing. He later had surgery to remove his kidney so he could give it to a compatible candidate. There are 90,000 people on the national transplant list, fewer than 17,000 receive one each year, and about 4,500 die waiting. The altruistic donor from Riverside, California, started the domino effect for thirty elective operations just like his. Sixty lives, thirty kidneys, all linked.[16]

What would our world look like if we all ruthlessly pursued significance first? What if we were so determined to make people's lives better that it influenced every decision we made? What if we prioritized others' needs the same way we prioritize our own?

Craig Altman is my pastor in Tampa and he asked me to golf with him on a Friday. Yes, the busiest day of my week, the day that had always made me the most money, the day I had never taken off before. Apprehensively, I went. I went despite the tasks I felt I needed to oversee and the availability I needed

---

15   "The pizza shop that pays it forward with compassion," *Upworthy*, February 27, 2015, https://www.youtube.com/watch?v=brzjeICcIt0.

16   Kevin Sack, "60 Lives, 30 Kidneys, All Linked," *The New York Times*, February 18, 2012, http://www.nytimes.com/2012/02/19/health/lives-forever-linked-through-kidney-transplant-chain-124.html?_r=2&src=me&ref=general.

to have. And it was game-changing: the fresh air, the edifying conversation, and the learning of patience and humility that only comes with the game of golf. From that day forward, I decided that I would do what my pastor did and take three people golfing every Friday.

Fostering relationships and dedicating quality time to friends old and new, coworkers past and present, and family members young and old was a far more enriching life path than being steeped in self and blinded by numbers. It wasn't about skipping out on my work responsibilities; it was about reevaluating their importance.

Priorities aren't what we say they are—they're revealed by what we actually do.

For fifteen years, Mark Richt was the beloved head football coach at the University of Georgia. On the field, he led the team to two conference championships, six division titles, and nine bowl games. Off the field, he was devoted to what he called "the Georgia Way," a philosophy based on winning with integrity and turning out players who can excel in life.

While in Georgia, he set up the Paul Oliver Network—named after the Georgia defensive back who killed himself after his professional career ended—to connect former players with his own contacts in the business community. He honored scholarships for players who got injured before they could matriculate at UGA. He refused to set scholarship restrictions that would have prevented players who left his football program from suiting up at rival schools. When other coaches were surveyed about who they'd like their own sons to play for, Mark Richt came in tied for first.

In 2015, the Georgia Bulldogs were favored to win their division. When they fell short of the championship, Richt was dismissed as the head coach. Though he was immediately offered the head coaching position at his alma mater, the University of Miami, the goodbye was a bittersweet end to an era. He had his team gather in the locker room so he could formally tell them he was leaving, but press reports had already leaked the news. When Coach Richt entered the room, he discovered that all the Georgia players were wearing Miami hats. When they saw him, they placed the tips of their thumbs together and held up "The U" sign, the famous hand signal for the University of Miami. Teary-eyed, Richt did it back to them.

He spoke to them about life and football and how proud he was of every man in that room. He told them he was still, and would always be, *for* them—no matter where he coached football. They could call him or come see him anytime. His door was never closed. Then he offered these final words to his players: "Life is about people, not rings. Rings collect dust."

At the end of our lives, our legacy won't be something we've achieved for ourselves. It will be the wake of people who have been impacted by our pursuit of purity in all things. It will be the choices we made and the leadership we exhibited. It will be what we did when no one was watching and how we picked ourselves up after falling. It will be our integrity that stood out in a world where the end justifies the means.

It will revolve around surrendering our personal gratification, believing in people more than they believe in themselves, setting our goals based on their goals, spending ten thousand hours mastering an expertise just so we can bless others with it, growing stronger so we can shoulder others' loads, and practicing what we preach. Because life is about people. Those we love and those we have yet to meet.

Challenge accepted.

CUT THE NOW

HEAD
WILL IT MATTER IN FIVE YEARS?

When it comes to your everyday life, there is always something competing for and requiring your attention—deadlines, kids, emails, dirty dishes, TV shows, exercising, date night—and even if your priorities are intact, even if you rationally know that your kids should win out over watching the newest episode of your favorite show, it's easy to feel lost and overwhelmed. And it's in those moments that you need to ask yourself whether what you're wrestling with today carries any real weight when it comes to accomplishing your long-term goals. Is what you're doing today setting you up for a better tomorrow? If you know where you're going and you know how you're getting there, the irrelevant minutiae can be given the perspective it deserves.

HEART

NEVER TRADE WHAT YOU WANT THE MOST FOR WHAT YOU WANT IN THE MOMENT.

June Carter Cash famously said, "I'm just trying to matter." You'd be hard-pressed to find someone who has zero desire to be remembered fondly or to leave the world better than how they found it. If you go one step further, you'll find that right underneath that desire is the layer that holds your motivation. Why do you want to matter? What do you want to mean to people? If you were defined by the successes of those who knew you, would you be known as selfish or selfless?

Leaving a legacy is all about the long term—investing your time and energy into what will matter when all is said and done. Being boxed in by the present is about the short term—not having the foresight to see that significance is built over time through countless decisions. That's not to say you shouldn't experience, enjoy, and savor the moment you're in. But it's about knowing that every action has a reaction and every cause has an effect. Every choice you make has an impact on other people, and it's up to you to make the right ones.

HANDS
TAKE MATTERS INTO YOUR OWN.

- What does success mean to you? How would you define it?

- What are your one-, five-, and ten-year plans? Are you on the right track to get there?

- When is the last time you were generous without giving money?

- List three personal values or traits that you hope are said about you during your eulogy. Are those aspirational or realistic?

- Look in the mirror. Do you have any regrets from today? How can you turn them around tomorrow?

FINAL WORDS

I hope this book was more than just a book. My desire was for *Red Key Revolution* to be a catalyst for becoming exactly who God created you to be. You have the ability to impact more lives than you could ever imagine.

It's time now to write the rest of *your* story. You will make decisions every day that will affect people you meet tomorrow. Choose to intentionally pursue significance and success. Cuts will be necessary for anything worthwhile, but when you sacrifice for what matters most, I promise it will be worth it.

You made it to the end of my first book. You trusted me with your time. You believed in me, the *tweener.* Thank you. If we ever meet, promise me a hug! Until then, my prayer is that your life would be rich with success in a way that leaves a legacy—the kind of success that will matter long after you're gone.

Live every day like someone else is counting on you, because someone always is.

Your friend,
Jordan

EPILOGUE

by Kristen Kemper

What you're about to read is my truth. Well, a glimpse of it anyway. Where I was in life and the cuts I needed to make in order to get where I longed to go. How I looked inward and upward to hone those cuts so they would unlock what they were meant to unlock. What (and who) was waiting for me when my keys were able to finally open the door. What you're about to read is what led up to the fruition of this revolution.

* * *

I always think back to the fact that a little over a year before I met Jordan, he wouldn't have been interested in me, and I wouldn't have been interested in him. Funny how timing works, isn't it?

In 2013, I was going through the motions of life, living it my way, doing what the world told me would make me happy and satisfied—except I wasn't. Have you ever felt that way? Like you're constantly striving and chasing those things? Looking at your life and feeling like you really should feel more content than you are, but there's still this longing in your heart? An emptiness that can't be filled, no matter how hard you try? If so, you're not alone. Awareness is the first element of change, and I finally woke up to the reality that I was chasing things that were insignificant. That deep contentment I had been long-ing for was met with the most overwhelming love I had ever known. God was calling me to so much more than the life I had been settling for, and it was time for me to make a change. His grace didn't just cover me, it changed me. It empowered and compelled me into action. I left my job at a good-paying high-end bar and my boyfriend of four years. I was completely surrendered, completely afraid, but completely sure that God is who He says He is and I could trust Him. While my story up to this point felt like a mess with a million broken pieces, it wasn't over, and it was time for a plot twist.

Throughout this time I started to ask myself some import-ant questions: What kind of woman do I want to be? Who do I want to impact? Since my future kids will be influenced more by what I do than what I say, what example do I want to set for them? What kind of wife do I want to be? I got clear about the kind of man I wanted to marry—the qualities that were need-to-have versus nice-to-have. Too often we're looking for something we aren't willing to be ourselves. What did I need to work on in order to be the best version of me? What were my need-to-haves?

This was all happening during a new and busy season of life that had me going to school full-time, working, mentor-ing some younger girls, leading and attending different small groups, and serving in different organizations. My head was down, my heart was growing, and my plate was full. Enter a friend of a friend on social media.

Over the course of eight months or so, a guy named Jordan followed me on my different social channels and would occasionally like or comment on something I'd post. We corresponded a handful of times through private messaging, but he wasn't on my radar as anything more than a friendly acquaintance. He eventually asked for my phone number, and I gave it to him, hesitantly. A day later, my phone rang, and it was him. I'll admit, I was a little caught off guard, yet was impressed with his boldness. I was expecting maybe a text message, but I didn't expect him to pick up the phone and ask me, a stranger, what my story is. It was disarming how genuine he seemed, and I decided to answer his questions with transparency and openness. About once a month he would send a text to me or call to check in and see how things were going in my world, but nothing more.

As my college graduation neared, I felt pulled to serve in Haiti and Uganda with two nonprofits started by friends of mine. Having recently given up my comfortable paycheck for a lesser-paying job, I set up a website where people could donate and listed the "fundraise goal" as one combined amount for both trips. The night before my Haiti amount was due, I was short by a decent amount of money and had no idea what I was going to do. I was sitting in the bathtub and got an alert through my phone that Jordan Kemper had donated. I read the amount. It was the *exact* amount I needed for the next day, down to the penny. Since the goal on my website was shown as one lump sum for two trips, he would have had no way of knowing how much I needed for Haiti specifically, or its deadline. Floored, I texted Jordan a thank-you, and he was completely casual about it in a simple text back.

I met Jordan in person a few months after I returned from Haiti. He said he was coming to Florida to visit some friends, but asked if we could hang out for a couple days beforehand. I agreed but had major second thoughts when the day arrived. I had so much going on, I hardly knew the guy, it was probably going to be weird, I hadn't thought it through. What had I gotten myself into?

I showed up to his hotel late and disheveled with no makeup on. A week of graduation celebrations was coming to an end, and I looked as exhausted as I felt. The last thing I was trying to do was impress him, and it showed. He accompanied me through two packed days of prior engagements, and then just the two of us had dinner the night before he was due to leave. Afterward, he asked if I wanted to take a walk on the beach. I thought that seemed a little too romantic—what if he tried to hold my hand?—so I said the first thing that popped into my head. "No . . . I don't like getting sand in my shoes." As someone who is rarely at a loss for words, I still can't believe that's the best response I could come up with. Sure, a walk on the beach may not seem like a critical, loaded decision, but I was cognizant of both the impression it might give and the implications of where it might lead. I thanked him for a nice time and said goodbye, glad that I had made a new friend.

I was heading to Seattle a couple weeks later with my parents—who are divorced, but have a good relationship and run a company together—for a business conference. Jordan said his sister lived there and that he had been intending to visit, so he asked if he could fly out and spend some time with me. This guy was certainly persistent—yet, not even close to pushy. A hard balance to strike.

I headed to Seattle, skeptical, while also curious. That first night he asked if I wanted to go for a walk on the pier, and I found myself saying yes. Had he started to grow on me? After we said goodnight, I wrestled with my thoughts in the elevator on the way back to my room. This was not a part of my plan, and the timing wasn't right.

My original life plan—graduate college, begin a career, be open to a serious relationship, start dating, get married, have kids. My updated life plan—be content being single and trust God with my future. I was not in a hurry to fall in love and was in less of a hurry to fall for someone I didn't know well—I was complete and content on my own, so what's the rush?

We went out to dinner on our final night in Seattle, and it was the biggest turning point in our relationship. While I resisted the timing of all of this, I was clear on the kind of man I wanted to marry one day, and I couldn't deny that Jordan was lining up on every front. I was continually asking difficult questions, sifting through the words he said and watching the way he acted and treated those around him. Then he told me the story that moved my heart in a way I didn't expect or even know was possible—he told me the story of his red key. He told me he hadn't shared that story with anyone before, and while I was honored that he chose to tell me, I felt the walls I had carefully built around my heart start to quickly crumble.

Hearing his story—what it meant to him and how he had been picturing the day where he could tell his future father-in-law, "I honored your daughter, and I waited for her"—opened my heart to the fact that this man was remarkably different. He was strong, but sweet. Steadfast and solid. He said what he meant and meant what he said. He was honest and confident in a totally unassuming way. He never pushed. He only asked and offered. Was it possible that he was exactly how he seemed? My ever-stubborn heart let go of its timeline, let down the walls, and when I went to bed that night, I thought to myself, *I think I'm going to marry this man.*

It's been years since that Seattle trip, and over two years since I took his last name. My observations about his character have been proven true time and time again. There was never a sudden reveal where it turned out Jordan was just putting his best foot forward; these attributes were innate to his character. The keys he talks about in this book are lived out by him on a daily basis. He's a true servant of others, including me, and consistently puts our needs before his own, celebrates our successes, shares in our sorrows, exercises forgiveness (like when he learned that I actually love getting sand in my shoes . . .), and leads with integrity. His belief that there's nothing more valuable than what you do for others is front and center in how he lives his life. To be loved by a man who chose to honor and love me before he even knew me is a Christlike love that is as transformative as it is humbling. The depth of what that has meant to me and what it's done for our marriage is something to which words could never do justice.

Regardless of what your beliefs are, know this: You are valued. You are loved. You are made with purpose and for a purpose. You have the opportunity to draw a line in the sand and make a decision that you're going to live the kind of story that you want to tell. One that inspires, one that redeems, one that impacts, one you're proud of, and one that lives on long after you're gone. I can tell you with confidence that what you've felt while reading this book is real. Ultimately, those feelings represent the realest you, the most impactful you, wanting to come out.

Let *that you* out. You were made for this.

GET YOUR KEY.
BEGIN YOUR STORY.

Gift Keys To Your Loved Ones, Too!
RedKeyRevolution.com

UNLOCK SIGNIFICANCE
SUCCESS THAT LASTS
with Jordan & Kristen Kemper

eCourse includes:

7 video lessons and 7 worksheets

For Individual and Group

Visit UnlockSignificance.com to learn more.

ABOUT THE AUTHOR

After graduating from Wheaton College, Jordan Kemper decided to forego medical school to begin his journey of entrepreneurship. His passion for health and wellness led him to build his first company, which now serves more than ten thousand customers. He has traveled the world and appeared on stages before thousands of people with other inspirational experts such as Dr. Oz, Tony Robbins, Sir Richard Branson, and John C. Maxwell. Today, he spends much of his time consulting for growing companies and speaking. Originally a Midwest boy from Rockford, Illinois, he and his wife, Kristen, live in Tampa, Florida. They enjoy traveling, fishing, quality time with friends and family, and spending time at home with their dog, Ella.

JOIN THE REVOLUTION

Let's redefine success,
one story at a time,
one key at a time.

Follow @RedKeyRevolution for inspiring stories.
Hastag #TheRedKey for your story to be featured!

Connect with Jordan on:

JordanKemper.com